MICROSOFT® POWERPOINT 2000

Presentation Graphics with Impact

PRENTICE HALL
Upper Saddle River, NJ 07458

Library of Congress Cataloging-in-Publication Data

Microsoft PowerPoint 2000: presentation graphics with impact/Against
The Clock
        p.   cm.
  ISBN 0-13-012639-X
  1. Computer Graphics 2. Microsoft PowerPoint (Computer file) 3.
Business presentataions--Graphic methods--Computer programs.
I. Against The Clock (Firm)
T385.M522257 2000

006.6' 869--dc21

Acquisitions Editor: *Elizabeth Sugg*	Formatting/page make-up: *Against The Clock, Inc.*
Developmental Editor: *Judy Casillo*	Printer/Binder: *Banta*
Supervising Manager: *Mary Carnis*	Cover Design: *Joe Sengotta*
Production Editor: *Denise Brown*	Icon Design: *James Braun*
Director of Manufacturing & Production: *Bruce Johnson*	Marketing Manager: *Shannon Simonsen*
Manufacturing Buyer: *Ed O'Dougherty*	Creative Director: *Marianne Frasco*
Editorial Assistant: *Brian Hyland*	Sales Director: *Ryan DeGrote*
	Director of Marketing: *Debbie Yarnell*

©2000 by Prentice Hall, Inc.
Upper Saddle River, New Jersey 07458

Printed in the United States of America

10 9 8 7 6 5 4 3 2 1

ISBN 0-13-012639-X

Prentice Hall International (UK) Limited, London
Prentice Hall of Australia Pty. Limited, Sydney
Prentice Hall Canada Inc., Toronto
Prentice Hall Hispanoamericana, S.A., Mexico
Prentice Hall of India Private Limited, New Delhi
Prentice Hall of Japan, Inc., Tokyo
Pearson Education Asia Pte. Ltd., Singapore
Editora Prentice Hall do Brasil, Ltda., Rio de Janeiro

Contents

PURPOSE

The Against The Clock series has been developed specifically for those involved in the field of graphic arts.

Welcome to the world of electronic design and prepress. Many of our readers are already involved in the industry — in advertising and design companies, in prepress and imaging firms, and in the world of commercial printing and reproduction. Others are just now preparing themselves for a career somewhere in the profession.

This series of courses will provide you with the skills necessary to work in this fast-paced, exciting, and rapidly expanding business. Many people feel that they can simply purchase a computer, the appropriate software, a laser printer, and a ream of paper, and begin designing and producing high-quality printed materials. While this might suffice for a barbecue announcement or a flyer advertising a local hair salon, the real world of four-color printing and professional communications requires a far more serious commitment.

THE SERIES

The applications presented in the Against The Clock series stand out as the programs of choice in professional graphic arts environments.

We've used a modular design for the Against The Clock series, allowing you to mix and match the drawing, imaging, and page layout applications that exactly suit your specific needs.

Titles available in the Against The Clock series include:

Macintosh: Basic Operations
Windows: Basic Operations
Adobe Illustrator: Introduction and Advanced Digital Illustration
Macromedia FreeHand: Introduction and Advanced Digital Illustration
Adobe PageMaker: Introduction and Advanced Electronic Mechanicals
QuarkXPress: Introduction and Advanced Electronic Mechanicals
Microsoft Publisher: Creating Electronic Mechanicals
Microsoft PowerPoint: Presentation Graphics with Impact
MetaCreations Painter: A Digital Approach to Natural Art Media
Adobe Photoshop: Introduction and Advanced Digital Images
Adobe Premiere: Digital Video Editing
Macromedia Director: Creating Powerful Multimedia
File Preparation: The Responsible Electronic Page
Preflight: An Introduction to File Analysis and Repair
TrapWise: Digital Trapping
PressWise: Digital Imposition

ICONS AND VISUALS

Pencil icon indicates a comment from an experienced operator. Whenever you see the pencil icon, you'll find corresponding sidebar text that augments or builds upon the subject being discussed at the time.

Bomb icon indicates a potential problem or difficulty. For instance, a certain technique might lead to pages that prove difficult to output. In other cases, there might be something that a program cannot easily accomplish, so we might present a workaround.

Pointing Finger indicates a hands-on activity — whether a short exercise or a complete project. This will be the icon you'll see the most throughout the course.

Key icon is used to point out that there is a keyboard equivalent to a menu or dialog-box option. Key commands are often faster than using the mouse to select a menu option. Experienced operators often mix the use of keyboard equivalents and menu/dialog box selections to arrive at their optimum speed.

CHAPTER OPENINGS *provide the reader with specific objectives.*

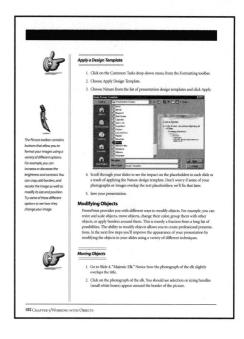

SIDEBARS and HANDS-ON ACTIVITIES *supplement concepts presented in the material.*

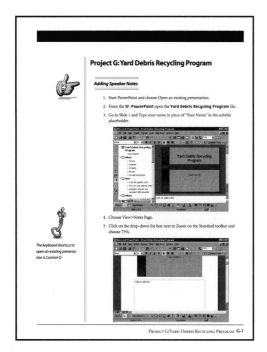

SUPPLEMENTAL PROJECTS *offer practice opportunities in addition to the exercises.*

PROJECT ASSIGNMENTS *will result in finished artwork — with an emphasis on proper file construction methods.*

The Against The Clock course materials have been constructed with two primary building blocks: exercises and projects. Projects always result in a finished presentation built from the ground up, with you creating all the elements within the scope of the specific assignment. This course, Microsoft PowerPoint: Presentation Graphics with Impact, makes use of several projects that you will work on during your learning sessions.

PROJECT A: THE BACKCOUNTRY ALMANAC

A presentation should be centered on a specific purpose. The Backcountry Almanac is a presentation designed to inform an audience about the essentials of surviving in the backcountry. In this project, you will use Microsoft PowerPoint to create and save a presentation, add slides, select slide layouts, add bullets and numbers, and switch views.

PROJECT B: FITNESS FACTS

The purpose of the Fitness Facts presentation is to inform the audience of the three keys to fitness and then persuade them to take action today. In this project, you will learn how to create a presentation using the AutoContent Wizard. In addition, you will copy slides from another presentation, delete slides, find and replace text, insert headers and footers, modify the slide master, rearrange the order of slides, and apply a design template.

PROJECT C: MASTERING GOLF

After your audience members see this presentation, they should be equipped with some tips and techniques that will enhance their golf game. While enhancing their golf game, you will be further enhancing your PowerPoint skills as you learn about promoting and demoting text in Outline view, changing the font and line spacing and using the Format Painter as well as cut, copy, and paste. You'll also learn about some marvelous enhancement tools such as text boxes and the Word Art application, which is used to apply special effects to text. Finally, you'll spell check your presentation. Spell checking provides further assurance that your presentation is professional and helps guarantee your credibility as a presenter.

PROJECT D: EASY & ELEGANT BAKING

An excellent way to add interest, variety and excitement to your presentation is to incorporate objects into your slides. Objects offer a creative way of visually communicating with your audience. A single graphic such as a photograph or chart can often illustrate what might take pages of text to address. To create this presentation, you'll insert clip art as well as photographs. You will also manipulate these objects by resizing, moving, copying, and rotating them as well as adding borders and fill effects to them. You'll also learn to create your own objects using the Drawing toolbar. In conclusion, you'll learn to align and group multiple objects.

PROJECT E: WILDFLOWER SPAS

The goal of this project is convince your audience members to treat themselves to a trip to Wildflower Spas. To persuade them to take advantage of the amenities offered, you will create this presentation from existing slides and imported text from a Microsoft Word document. You will incorporate and modify tables to organize the text used in this presentation. You will also enhance the tables by changing the column width and row height and adding borders and shading. To further enhance the presentation, you will make use of PowerPoint's transitions and animation effects. As a final touch, you'll prepare speaker's notes, which you'll use to remind yourself of important points that aren't included on the slides viewed by the audience.

PROJECT F: WASHINGTON APPLES ONLINE

The Web has become a popular and viable means of distributing information. PowerPoint makes it easy for you to save your presentations in an HTML format so that they can be distributed via the Web. You'll use PowerPoint to create an online business presence in this project. First, you'll save a presentation as a Web page. Next, you'll learn how to view both the slide show and HTML source code in your browser. In order to navigate your presentation nonlinearly and create cross-references within your presentation, you'll set objects and text as hyperlinks to slides, Web addresses, and email addresses. Once created, you will copy and edit these hyperlinks. Upon completion of this project, you should understand how to publish your presentations to a Web server to be viewed by the Internet community.

PROJECT G: YARD DEBRIS RECYCLING PROGRAM

Recycling is as important as delivering a professional presentation. This final project will teach you how to enhance the delivery of your presentation through the use of speaker's notes, transitions, and animation effects. In addition, you will feel more comfortable delivering your PowerPoint presentation once you know how to start a slide show on any slide and navigate to any slide at any time. You'll increase your credibility as a presenter when you use PowerPoint's pen tool and change screen features. In addition to learning about on-screen delivery, in this project you'll understand how and why you may want to print speaker's notes, outlines, and audience handouts.

FOR THE STUDENT

On the CD-ROM you will find a complete set of Against The Clock (ATC) fonts, as well as a collection of data files used to construct the various exercises and projects.

The ATC fonts are solely for use while you are working with the Against The Clock materials. These fonts will be used throughout both the exercises and projects.

A variety of student files have been included. These files are necessary to complete both the exercises and projects.

FOR THE INSTRUCTOR

The Instructor Kit consists of an Instructor's Manual and an Instructor's CD-ROM. It includes various testing and presentation materials in addition to the files that come standard with the student books.

- **Overhead Presentation Materials** are provided and follow along with the course. These presentations are prepared using Microsoft PowerPoint and are provided in both "native" PowerPoint format as well as Acrobat Portable Document Format (PDF).

- **Finished artwork (in PDF format)** for all projects that the students complete is supplied on the CD-ROM.

- **A Test Bank of Questions** is included on the instructor CD-ROM. These questions may be modified, reorganized, and administered throughout the delivery of the course.

- Halfway through the course is a **Review** of material covered to that point, with a **Final Review** at the end.

ACKNOWLEDGEMENTS

We would like to give special thanks the writers, editors, and others who have worked long and hard to complete the Against The Clock series. Foremost among them are Dean Bagley, Michael Barnett, and Alison O'Donnell, whom I thank for their long nights, early mornings, and their seemingly endless patience.

Thanks to the dedicated teaching professionals whose comments and expertise contributed to the success of these products, with a special thanks to Anna Ursyn of The University of Northern Colorado.

And to Michael Barnett, Copy Editor and final link in the chain of production, for his tremendous help in making sure we all said what we meant to say.

A big thanks to Judy Casillo, Developmental Editor, and Denise Brown, Production Editor, for their guidance, patience, and attention to detail.

Ellenn Behoriam, Series Editor

August, 1999

ABOUT AGAINST THE CLOCK

Against The Clock (ATC) was founded in 1990 as a part of Lanman Systems Group, one of the nation's leading systems integration and training firms. The company specialized in developing custom training materials for such clients as *L.L. Bean, The New England Journal of Medicine, Smithsonian,* the *National Education Association, Air & Space Magazine, Publishers Clearing House,* The *National Wildlife Society, Home Shopping Network,* and many others. The integration firm was among the most highly respected in the graphic arts industry.

To a great degree, the success of Systems Group can be attributed to the thousands of pages of course materials developed at the company's demanding client sites. Throughout the rapid growth of Systems Group, founder and General Manager Ellenn Behoriam developed the expertise necessary to manage technical experts, content providers, writers, editors, illustrators, designers, layout artists, proofreaders, and the rest of the chain of professionals required to develop structured and highly effective training materials.

Following the sale of the Lanman Companies to World Color, one of the nation's largest commercial printers, Ellenn embarked on a project to develop a library of training materials engineered specifically for the professional graphic artist. A large part of this effort is finding and working with talented professional artists, writers, and educators from around the country.

The result is the ATC training library.

ABOUT THE AUTHOR

Dr. Calleen Coorough has been teaching computers, technology education and application software for twelve years. She is currently teaching at Skagit Valley College in Mount Vernon, WA. Prior to coming to Skagit Valley College, she taught in Idaho at both Lewis-Clark State College and the University of Idaho. She has also provided training and consulting to businesses throughout Idaho, Washington, and Massachusetts.

At Skagit Valley College, Dr. Coorough teaches courses in Multimedia & Interactive Technology, Computer Information Systems, and Office & Business Technology including such classes as Introduction to the Internet, Introduction to Interactive Multimedia, Creating & Designing Web Pages, Photoshop, Multimedia Authoring, and a host of Microsoft Office classes. She is also a proponent of online education, distance learning, and virtual universities. As such, she has been teaching online education at Skagit Valley College since the summer of 1996 and has developed online curriculum for twelve different courses, which have been taught to over a thousand students throughout the state of Washington.

She has always been interested in multimedia, and as a result has been involved in the development of a multimedia certificate and degree focused on preparing Web-based multimedia applications.

GETTING STARTED

Platform

While the Against The Clock series is usually designed to apply to both Macintosh and Windows systems, Microsoft PowerPoint, at least at this time, runs under Windows only. As a result, there are no cross-platform incompatibilities to be concerned with.

Naming Conventions

In the old days of MS-DOS and Windows 3.x systems, file names on the PC were limited to something referred to as "8.3," which meant that you were limited in the number of characters you could use to an eight-character name (the "8") and a three-character extension (the "3"). Text files, for example, might be called *myfile.txt*, while a document file from a word processor might be called *myfile.doc* (for document). On today's Windows systems, these limitations have been overcome. Although you can use longer file names, extensions still exist. Whether you see them or not is another story.

When your system is first configured, the Views are normally set to a default that hides these extensions. This means that you might have a dozen different files named *myfile*, all of which may have been generated by different applications and consist of completely different types of files.

You can change this view by double-clicking on *My Computer* (the icon is on your desktop). Choose View>Folder Options. From Folder Options, select the View tab. Within the Files and Folders folder is a checkbox: "Hide file extensions for known file types." When this is unchecked, you can see the file extensions. It's easier to know what you're looking at if they're visible. While this is a personal choice, we strongly recommend viewing the file extensions. All the files used in this course have been named using the three-character extension.

Key Commands

There are two keys generally used as *modifier* keys — they do nothing when pressed unless they are pressed in conjunction with another key. Their purpose is to alter the normal functions of the key they are pressed in conjunction with.

The Control key is generally used when taking control of the computer. When combined with the "S" key, it functions to save your work. When combined with "O" it opens a file; with a "P" it prints the file. In addition to these functions, which work with most Windows programs, the Control key may be combined with other keys in PowerPoint to take control of specific functions.

The keys on the top row of the keypad, F1–F12 also accomplish specific tasks in conjunction with the computer. F1 will display the Help menu. F6 and Shift-F6 will move elements to the front or the back of a "stack" of text and graphic objects.

The CD-ROM and Initial Setup Considerations

Before you begin using your Against The Clock course book, you must set up your system to have access to the various files and tools to complete your lessons.

Student Files

This course comes complete with a collection of student files. These files are an integral part of the learning experience — they're used throughout the course to help you construct increasingly complex elements. Having these building blocks available to you for practice and study sessions will ensure that you will be able to experience the exercises and complete the project assignments smoothly using a minimum of time spent looking for the various required components.

In the Student Files folders, we've created sets of data. Locate the "**SF-PowerPoint**" folder and simply drag the icon onto your hard disk drive. If you have limited disk space, you may want to copy only the files for one or two lessons at a time.

Creating a Project Folder

We strongly recommend that you work from your hard disk. However, in some cases you might not have enough room on your system for all of the files that we've supplied or you may be working in a lab setting in which it is impossible to work from the hard disk. If this is the case, you can work directly from the CD-ROM.

Throughout the exercises and projects, you'll be required to save your work. Since the CD-ROM is "read-only," you cannot write information to it. Create a Project Folder on your hard disk and use it to store your work-in-progress. Create your project folder using Control-N while you're looking at your desktop. This will create the folder at the highest level of your system, where it will be easy to find. If you cannot leave the folder on the hard drive, you can copy it or files from it to a removable storage device. Name this folder "**Work in Progress**".

Fonts

The fonts that are called for during the hands-on activities throughout this course are either included within the ATC fonts folder or are prepackaged with Microsoft PowerPoint. If these fonts are not available on your computer, reinstall them from the enclosed CD-ROM or from your Microsoft PowerPoint or Office 2000 application CD-ROM.

System Requirements

If you are running a Windows operating system, you will need a 486 or Pentium-based processor; Windows 95/NT 4.0 and higher (performs under Windows 98); 16 MB RAM (32 recommended); Color Display (24 bit recommended); and CD-ROM drive.

Prerequisites

This book assumes that you have a basic understanding of how to use your system.

You should know how to use your mouse to point and click, and how to drag items around the screen. You should know how to resize a window, and how to arrange windows on your desktop to maximize your available space. You should know how to access pull-down menus and how checkboxes and radio buttons work. Lastly, you should know how to create, open, and save files.

If you're familiar with these fundamental skills, then you know all that's necessary to utilize the Against The Clock courseware library.

Notes:

INTRODUCTION

This course has been designed to familiarize you with the fundamental uses of Microsoft PowerPoint 2000. The course will prepare you to take and pass the Microsoft Office User Specialist (MOUS) exam at the proficient level. In addition, the course will provide you with some fundamental skills in preparing and delivering a presentation to an audience.

Microsoft PowerPoint 2000 is a presentation graphics program. You will use PowerPoint to create slide shows. There are many different ways to create and deliver PowerPoint slide shows. Slide shows can be presented to an audience by a speaker. They can be viewed and controlled by a user. They can be timed to run continuously on a computer used as a kiosk without being controlled by a speaker or user or they can be saved as Web pages and viewed from a Web browser via the Internet or an intranet.

PowerPoint is an incredibly versatile program. Regardless of the equipment and technology you have available, PowerPoint can help you deliver your message. If you don't have the computer equipment, projection systems or Internet access needed to deliver PowerPoint slide shows in one of the ways mentioned above, PowerPoint's additional features include the ability to convert your slide shows to transparencies for use on an overhead projector or to 35mm slides for use with a slide projector.

In addition to being versatile, PowerPoint 2000 is an easy program to learn and use. It's very intuitive. Design templates, wizards, text, clip art, graphs, charts, transitions, animation, and other media elements make it easy to create a professional presentation in no time. By making it easy to create and format a professional presentation, PowerPoint allows you to focus on the content of your message and polish your delivery.

If you are delivering your presentation in front of an audience, PowerPoint's ability to print speaker notes, outlines, and audience handouts can further assist you in your goals to effectively and professionally deliver your message. Speaker notes consist of a picture of the slide along with notes that you have prepared to accompany each slide. A printed outline gives you and your audience a quick overview of your entire presentation. Audience handouts print three to six miniature slides per page. These can be given to your audience as supplemental material or for note taking.

No matter how you choose to use PowerPoint, you will find it a fun, easy way to professionally share a message designed to inform, persuade, or simply entertain.

Notes:

CHAPTER 1

PREPARING YOUR PRESENTATION

CHAPTER OBJECTIVE:

To learn how to follow a sequence of stages that will help you prepare, organize, and deliver an effective presentation to your audience. To realize that the success of your presentation depends on the development of a purpose that is clearly stated and pervasive. In Chapter 1 you will:

- Define your purpose by establishing the type of information that will be most useful to your audience.

- Develop your presentation topic based on your purpose.

- Research your subject to develop an effective presentation.

- Analyze your audience so that you can tailor your presentation to meet its wants and needs.

- Support your points so that your audience will understand the connection between the facts and your purpose.

- Prepare an outline that organizes your content and prepares you to deliver a professional presentation.

- Use visual aids to involve the audience by giving them something to look at, touch, taste, or smell.

- Deliver your message by being prepared, natural in your speech, enthusiastic, honest, ethical, and credible.

Preparing Your Presentation

Preparation is the single most important element to being relaxed in front of a crowd. Before you create a PowerPoint presentation, you must plan and prepare. Doing so will improve the quality and effectiveness of your presentation. In addition, it will ultimately save you time. The more logical your speech is, the easier it is for you to learn and deliver. It is easy to prepare a speech once you know how to do it.

In this chapter, we will examine the various stages of preparing a presentation. At each stage, PowerPoint provides tools to help you create a more effective presentation. The remainder of this book will teach you how to use this fabulous presentation program so that you can become a powerful presenter.

Defining Your Purpose

When you prepare a presentation, your success depends on the development of a purpose that is clearly stated and pervasive. In attempting to develop your purpose, try to imagine why your audience might want or need the message you will be providing. Attempt to answer these questions:

What type of information will be most useful to the audience?

What will the audience gain from this presentation?

How might the audience members use what they gain?

How will the message be delivered?

Is the purpose of the presentation to entertain, to inform, or to persuade?

Does the occasion of the speech have a specific purpose?

There are many types of presentations. The type of presentation is dependent upon the speaker's intention. For example, a speaker may seek to inform, to persuade, to provide the basis for action, or to entertain.

To Inform: In an informative speech, the goal is to inform the audience about a new subject or to provide information about an already familiar subject. An informative purpose statement should focus on increasing audience knowledge or ability.

Most informative speeches provide information about objects, processes, events, or concepts. The goal of the speaker in an informative speech is to describe, explain, or instruct. Regardless of the goal, information presented to the audience should be new.

To Persuade: A persuasive speech is intended to change the attitudes, beliefs, or behavior of the audience. The persuasive speech can be quite challenging because it is often centered on controversial subjects that are important to both the speaker and the audience.

In a persuasive speech, you attempt to persuade your audience by using either a proposition of fact, value, or policy. With a proposition of fact, you present the facts from two or more conflicting viewpoints and allow your audience to choose the truth based on the facts you present. Using a proposition of value, you explore the merit or value of an object, person, or idea. You may choose to take a proposition of value beyond exploration by recommending that your audience adopt a specific course of action. This type of speech is often referred to as a proposition of policy.

To Entertain: A speech to entertain attempts to gain and keep the audience's attention. The speaker wants the audience to enjoy themselves, to be amused, or be interested in the content of the presentation.

Once you have developed a clear purpose, the AutoContent Wizard in PowerPoint can help you break the purpose down into a deliverable message. You'll learn more about the AutoContent Wizard when you create your first PowerPoint presentation in Chapter 2.

Developing Your Topic

A clear understanding of your purpose should help you select a topic. In fact, the purpose and the topic will be intertwined. The earlier you decide on a topic, the more time you'll have to prepare a quality presentation. Speakers with a topic in mind will begin generating ideas for their presentation based on what they see or hear around them. What they observe will inevitably provide inspiration for their speech.

If your topic isn't provided for you, you'll need to come up with a topic that helps you meet the purpose of your presentation. In order for you to generate enthusiasm and inspire audience interest in your topic, it's important that you also be interested in the topic. Your interest in a topic will improve your ability to prepare the presentation, and will increase your confidence when it comes time to present.

One way to find something that interests you and your audience is to draw from your personal interests as well as those of your audience members. It's also wise to choose a familiar topic. As a speaker, you want your audience to perceive you as credible and qualified to speak about your topic.

In deciding upon a topic, ask yourself the following questions:

Am I interested in the topic?

Will I enjoy talking about this topic?

Will the audience be interested in this topic?

Will the topic offend members of the audience?

Do I know something about this topic?

Do I have any interest in learning about this topic?

Researching Your Subject

Before you can deliver an effective presentation, you must know your subject. If necessary, you should conduct research to prepare for the presentation. Research will generally increase your speech effectiveness as well as enhance your credibility. Knowledge of controversies and the latest information will help you anticipate the audience's attitudes and will assist you in developing strategies to deal with them.

There are many different ways to conduct research for your topic. Today, the Internet provides one means for researching your subject. In addition to the billions of Web sites available, you may also find useful information through e-mail, newsgroups, or electronic bulletin boards.

You can also draw from the more traditional forms of media including newspapers, magazines, radio, and television. A visit to a local community or college library may be in order. Visiting your local library offers the potential advantage of assistance from a reference librarian.

At times, personal interviews may also prove helpful. Interviews can be used to collect facts and to stimulate or clarify ideas. Sometimes, the interview is the best way to uncover information that isn't available in any other format. Interviews are particularly helpful for information gathering because they allow you to see your topic from an expert's perspective. Interviewing an expert allows you to take advantage of that expert's experience, research, and opinions.

Analyzing Your Audience

In addition to knowing your subject, you must also know your audience. The more you know about your audience, the more you can tailor your presentation to meet its wants and needs. This should be your goal. Your audience members are the reason for your presentation, and as such, they are the key to your presentation's success. If you don't consider your audience, your presentation is likely to be a flop.

Analyzing your audience will help you prepare a message that your listeners will respond to in a positive manner. Whenever possible, you should attempt to determine your listeners' values, beliefs, likes, and dislikes.

You should also analyze the demographics of your audience. Demographic data tells you about group, not individual, characteristics. As such, the validity of this type of information is sometimes questionable; however, it can help you prepare a presentation that more appropriately matches your audience in general. Demographic data includes:

- Age

- Occupation

- Religion

- Ethnic or cultural background

- Social or economic status

- Gender

- Educational background

- Political background

The more clearly you can see your presentation through the eyes of your audience, the more successful your presentation will be. This is particularly important if you wish to motivate your audience. You must consider its needs and desires. In analyzing your audience, find answers to the following questions:

Who are my audience members?

What are the demographics of my audience?

What particular interests, beliefs, and values do my audience members have in common?

What particular aspects of the topic will be most relevant to them?

How can I best gain and hold their interest and attention?

What do I share in common with my listeners?

How can I build on this common ground?

What might be the audience's reaction to my presentation?

What will my listeners already know about my topic?

What will they want to know?

What do they need to know?

Is the information geared to their level?

Is the language appropriate for this audience?

In addition to analyzing your audience so that you can tailor your presentation to meet its needs and expectations, you must also be empathic toward your audience during the presentation. For example, if you use unfamiliar terms or a particular term in an unfamiliar way, be certain to explain it to your audience. You should also explain all acronyms. Don't assume that your audience knows what you mean.

Time constraints are also an important consideration. If your audience expects you to speak for twenty minutes, you should only speak for twenty minutes. If you're presenting in the morning, you may need to begin with a startling example that will awaken your audience. If your presentation is on Friday, you should probably be more direct in order to keep listeners' minds from wandering to the weekend.

To prepare a message that is suited to your audience, you should follow these general guidelines:

- Use short sentences.

- Read a local newspaper or magazine.

- Watch the local news for current or upcoming events.

- Research the group to which you plan to speak.

- For a receptive audience, focus on conclusions and recommendations.

- For a skeptical audience, focus on logical arguments.

Supporting Your Points

You will be a more credible speaker if you can support your message. Therefore, it is important that your presentation be well supported. Supporting material is used to clarify, make interesting, make memorable, or to prove a point. There are several techniques that you can use to support your message.

Descriptive statistics can be used to explain the size or distribution of your topic. Statistics are powerful because they imply that they are the result of a thorough scientific study. In evaluating statistics, consider the source, completely cite the source, and use only current and relevant statistics. It's also a good idea to seek out multiple statistics to support your point.

Stories or narratives can also serve as support for your message. Audiences will often listen to and believe a story before they will believe statistics. When telling a story, be certain that your audience understands the connection between the story and the point that you are trying to make. This connection should be obvious. To make an impact, the story must also be interesting. To keep the story interesting, avoid unnecessary details and excessive length.

It may be necessary to provide your audience with definitions that support your point. There are different types of definitions, including dictionary definitions, descriptions, and operational definitions.

Using humor may help your audience identify with and remember your topic. Obviously, humor should not be used under any and all circumstances. However, when used appropriately, humor can actually help build your credibility.

Testimonials made by experts can also help you support your position. Testimonials are most effective and appropriate with persuasive speeches, but they can be effectively incorporated into any type of speech.

Outlining Your Points

Once your purpose has been defined, and your topic and audience have been researched and analyzed, it's time to organize your presentation. One way to organize your presentation is to prepare an outline. A speech is like architecture, and the outline serves as a blueprint of your presentation. By hierarchically organizing your content into primary, secondary, and tertiary topics, you will be better prepared to produce a professional presentation. PowerPoint offers an Outline View specifically for this purpose.

A presentation that is well outlined will have a natural flow. Outlining your points will help you identify key topics. It will also enable you to easily add to your presentation as you go. Though you can write an outline in complete sentences, it is probably best to limit the outline to key words and phrases.

One simple method for developing the body of your speech is to divide it into three main points. Choose the three main points from the three aspects of your topic that provide the most interesting information. Research has shown that using three points seems to be pleasing to most audiences.

Don't overwhelm the audience with too much information. You can't tell an audience everything there is to know about your topic in one speech, so don't try.

There are different methods or organizational patterns that can be used to outline your points. Regardless of which method you choose, be certain that all of your points support the goal and purpose of the speech.

Topical: One organizational pattern that can be used when you have several ideas to present and one idea seems to precede the others, is the topical method. This is one of the most common types of patterns, and it is especially useful for speeches designed to inform or entertain.

Chronological: If your presentation seems to have a logical time sequence, consider using a chronological organization method. This method is useful in speeches to inform or persuade because both of these types of speeches often require background information.

Spatial: You should use this method if you are able to organize your material according to physical space. This organization method can be used for both speeches to inform and speeches to entertain.

Classification: This common organizational pattern requires that you categorize your points. Classification can be used with all three types of speeches.

Problem/Solution: This method of organizing a speech is most often used in speeches to persuade, where the first part of the speech outlines a problem and the second part presents a solution.

Cause/Effect: Though this method of organization is often used for persuasive speeches, it can certainly be effective for any type of speech. The first part of the speech describes the cause of a problem and the second describes its effect.

In addition to the body of the speech, every good presentation should also have an effective introduction and conclusion. A good introduction will provide an interesting start to the speech. It's important that the audience learn up front how they are going to benefit from listening to your presentation.

There are several ways to begin your presentation. You can ask a question, state an unusual or startling fact, direct audience attention to a visual aid, or tell them an interesting story or personal experience. A good introduction can also build speaker confidence, which will help you relax and deliver a more effective presentation.

Introductions should be designed to:

- Gain the attention of the audience.

- Introduce the topic.

- Illustrate the importance of the topic.

- Present the purpose.

- Forecast the main points.

Just as you need to prepare an effective introduction, you also need to give your audience a more worthwhile conclusion than "That's it," or "I guess I'm done." Conclusions such as these are too abrupt. Instead, you should close your presentation with information.

The conclusion should:

- Inform the audience that you are about to close.

- Summarize the main points.

- Leave the audience with something to remember.

Using Visual Aids

There are many reasons to incorporate visual aids into your presentation. Some of the more predominant are that visual aids:

- Grab and keep audience attention by giving your audience something to look at, touch, smell, or taste.

- Involve the audience to a much greater extent than if they were just listening to your speech.

- Enhance audience understanding.

- Add a sense of reality.

- Add variety.

- Give your presentation lasting impact — the more of the audience's senses (sight, sound, touch, smell, taste) you can stimulate during your speech, the longer and more vividly the audience will remember the information.

- Help to build your credibility.

- Save time — information on charts and graphs often makes it easier and faster to explain content. Pictures and props make lengthy verbal descriptions unnecessary.

- Help to control nervousness — the use of visual aids often takes the focus away from the speaker and therefore eases nervousness.

Visual aids stimulate the senses — smell, touch, and taste. There are a variety of items that can be used as visual aids. PowerPoint slides and materials are visual aids. In addition, you will discover in the chapters that follow, that PowerPoint allows you to include different types of visual aids directly into your presentation. When preparing your PowerPoint presentation, consider incorporating the following types of visual aids:

- Sketches

- Maps

- Graphs: pie, bar, line

- Flowcharts

- Organizational charts

- Photographs and pictures

- Objects

- Sound

- Animation

- Video

- Posters

- Video tapes

- Audio tapes

- Slides

- Live props: animals, pets, humans

In preparing your visual aids, consider these pointers:

- Use visual aids to supplement the speech, not replace it.

- Design visual aids that are balanced and pleasing to the eye.

- Add color that impacts and coincides with the meaning of the speech.

- Use visual aids that emphasize what the speech is attempting to emphasize.

- Create relevant and simple visual aids.

- Use readable font sizes — 24 pt. for titles; 18 pt. for subtitles; 14 pt. for other text.

- Display your visual aids slowly.

- Display your visual aids so that they don't interfere with your eye contact or muffle your voice; don't hold them directly in front of your face.

Delivering Your Message

Though you may prepare a PowerPoint presentation that will be delivered online as a Web page via the Internet or running endlessly as part of a kiosk, more often than not you will use your PowerPoint presentation to deliver a speech before an audience. This is the point at which all of your hard work and preparation comes together.

There are different delivery formats that will guide how your message is delivered. Some of the more common formats include impromptu, extemporaneous, manuscript, and memorized. Though your delivery will vary depending upon the format, the guidelines below should help you effectively deliver your content:

- Be prepared

- Be natural

- Be appropriate

- Be enthusiastic

- Be honest

- Be ethical

- Be credible

The importance of practice cannot be overemphasized. The more you practice, the more prepared and confident you will become. Practice in front of a mirror or practice in front of friends and family. You might also want to consider joining a group such as Toastmasters. If possible, you should practice in the environment where you will be giving the presentation and use the equipment that will be available during your speech.

There is more to speaking than just saying words. While the audience is listening to you, they are also watching your hands, facial expressions, and body language. Don't become a robot.

Nonverbal communication is an important part of presenting. Research has proven that if your nonverbal communication does not coincide with what you are saying, your audience will believe what they see. Consequently, you need to make certain that your nonverbal communication reinforces your verbal communication. Here are some points to recognize:

- Eye contact will make you appear more credible.

- Use vocal variety. Nothing will put an audience to sleep faster than a monotone speaker. The most effective tone, and one that is the most pleasant for the audience to listen to, is a conversational tone. Your goal is to have a conversation with your audience.

- Appropriate movement will help emphasize points and involve the audience.

- Nonverbal communication aids audience understanding. Facial expressions and body language also help demonstrate emotions such as surprise, anger, fatigue or sadness.

- Gestures help entertain your audience. Use gestures to act out the speech.

- Use nonverbal communication to help you relax. If you don't use natural gestures, your nervous energy will often surface as a distracting mannerism.

- Your posture is important in determining how the audience perceives you. While making a presentation, avoid leaning against the wall or slouching on the podium. Stand erect and hold your head high. Good posture will also give you better voice projection.

When using visual aids to assist you in the delivery of your message, consider the following:

- Be certain that your visual aids are integrated into your speech.

- Test electronic equipment before you begin.

- Practice using electronic equipment.

- Only display an introductory slide until you are ready to begin.

- When your presentation has concluded, display a blank slide to keep the audience from becoming distracted.

- Do not stand directly in front of your visual aids; stand to the side and face the audience as much as possible.

- When referring to your visual aid, point, if necessary; do not leave your audience searching.

- Distribute materials before or after your presentation; do not distribute them during your presentation.

With planning, preparation, practice, and PowerPoint, you'll be on your way to creating an effective presentation. The following chapters will teach you to use this wonderful presentation tool to deliver a powerful presentation.

CHAPTER 2

CREATING A PRESENTATION

CHAPTER OBJECTIVE:

To understand the mechanics and the use of PowerPoint's tools to create an effective presentation. You will learn how to use PowerPoint's AutoLayouts such as Title Slide, Bulleted List, Text & Clip art, Text & Chart, Text & Media Clip, and Object Only. In Chapter 2 you will:

- Become familiar with the PowerPoint Working Environment.

- Learn to create a blank presentation and add slides by first choosing an AutoLayout from the New Slide dialog box.

- Learn how to save, close, and open a presentation.

- Navigate among different views (slide, outline, sorter, normal, slide show) and learn how each view serves a slightly different purpose.

- Apply a design template which is a preset format that includes the colors and appearance of the background, as well as the type style of the titles, subtitles, and other text included in your presentation.

- Use the AutoContent Wizard to create or modify a presentation.

PROJECTS TO BE COMPLETED:

- **The Backcountry Almanac**
- Fitness Facts
- Mastering Golf
- Easy & Elegant Baking
- Wildflower Spas
- Washington Apples Online
- Yard Debris Recycling Program

Creating a Presentation

The PowerPoint Working Environment

Many of the elements found in Microsoft PowerPoint are also common to other Microsoft Office and Windows programs. At the top of the screen you'll find a blue Title bar that indicates that you that you are running the PowerPoint application. It also displays the name of the presentation that is currently open. If you have not yet named your presentation, it will be listed as Presentation1. To the right of the Title bar are the document control menu buttons, also known as the Minimize, Maximize, Restore, and Close buttons. Below the Title bar is the Menu bar. You can access commands from the Menu bar by either clicking on the command and choosing another command from the list of options, or by holding down the Alt key and pressing the underlined letter. For example, to bring up the commands from the Format menu, hold down Alt-O. Go ahead and try it now. To remove the menu from the screen, either press the Esc key or click anywhere outside of the menu.

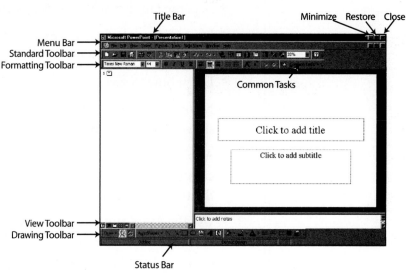

Below the Menu bar is the Standard toolbar. The Standard toolbar contains icons representing shortcuts to some of the most commonly used commands available on the Menu bar. If you position your mouse pointer over one of the icons on the toolbar, a ToolTip or yellow box containing the name of the icon will appear. Under the Standard toolbar is the Formatting toolbar. This toolbar is aptly named because it contains icons or buttons that help you format your presentation.

At the bottom of your screen, on the left-hand side, you'll find a small toolbar that has five different buttons that allow you to change the way you view a presentation. This is the View toolbar. Each of these views is useful depending upon what you are trying to do in PowerPoint. You can switch views by clicking on the appropriate view button on the View toolbar. The current view will be displayed in the Status bar at the bottom of the screen. In addition, the button or icon of the current view appears to be depressed or pushed in.

The Formatting toolbar may appear to the right of the Standard toolbar instead of beneath it. To move it, position your mouse pointer on the double-vertical line to the left of the Font drop-down list box until the mouse changes to a four-headed arrow. Drag the Formatting toolbar down and release the mouse.

Below the View toolbar you'll find the Drawing toolbar. The Drawing toolbar contains a collection of tools used to create and edit drawing objects such as rectangles, circles, and lines. Below the Drawing toolbar is the Status bar. In general, the left side of the Status bar displays the number of the current slide as well as the total number of slides in the presentation, and the right side displays the name of the design template.

In addition to the toolbars mentioned above, the three most commonly used tasks in PowerPoint are available from the Common Tasks drop down menu on the Formatting toolbar. These tasks include inserting a new slide, choosing a slide layout, and applying a design template.

Creating Your First PowerPoint Presentation

When you start PowerPoint, the first screen you encounter requires that you specify whether or not you wish to open an existing presentation or create a new presentation using the AutoContent Wizard, Template, or Blank Presentation.

Wizards automate an operation through the use of a series of steps or dialog boxes that ask you questions. The AutoContent Wizard walks you through a series of questions that help you create a presentation. Using this wizard, you can choose from a list of presentation categories. In addition, you select a style for your presentation, the appearance of handouts, and the method of output. Upon completion of this series of question, the wizard generates an outline with sample text. The next step is to replace the sample text with your own.

A template is a preset design feature that gives all of the slides in a presentation a similar appearance. Using a design template gives your presentation a consistent design, color scheme, and font.

Start PowerPoint

1. Click on the Start button in the lower-left corner of the taskbar.

2. From the Start menu, point to Programs and look for Microsoft Office or Microsoft PowerPoint.

3. Click on Microsoft PowerPoint to start the program.

Microsoft PowerPoint may also be listed as PowerPoint or PowerPoint 2000.

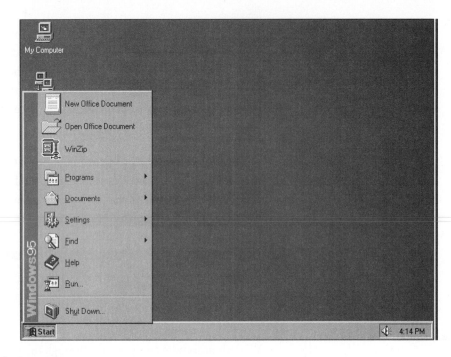

Slide Layouts

When you create a new PowerPoint presentation or add a new slide to an existing presentation, you must first choose an AutoLayout from the New Slide dialog box. PowerPoint includes many different slide layouts. These layouts allow you to select a slide arrangement that matches the content you plan to include on the slide. The slide layouts include placeholders for titles, text, graphics, organizational charts, and media clips.

To help you choose the appropriate layout, PowerPoint includes both a preview of the placeholders included in the layout as well as the name of the layout. Click on any of the AutoLayouts. The name of the layout appears in the lower-right corner of the dialog box.

Some of the more common AutoLayouts include:

- Title slide

- Bulleted list

- Text & clip art

- Text & chart

- Text & media clip

- Object only

In addition to choosing a layout whenever you add a new slide to a presentation, you can also change the layout of a slide at any time. To change the layout, simply click on the Slide Layout button on either the Standard toolbar or from Common Tasks on the Formatting toolbar. You don't need to worry about losing the content on the existing slide. PowerPoint will merely reposition the text and graphics into suitable placeholders using the new layout.

To apply an AutoLayout in Slide view, Choose Format>Slide Layout or click the Slide Layout button on the Standard toolbar. You can also right-click the slide and select Slide Layout from the Shortcut menu or choose Slide Layout from the Common Tasks drop-down menu on the Formatting toolbar. When the Slide Layout dialog box appears, click the desired layout and choose Apply.

Create a Blank Presentation and Choose Slide Layouts

1. At the dialog box, choose Blank presentation.

2. The New Slide dialog box displays a list of the available AutoLayouts for your slide. Choose Title Slide and click OK.

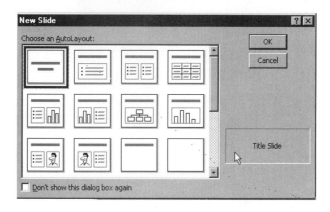

3. Your Title Slide should now be displayed in Normal view. Switch to Slide view by clicking on the Slide View button on the Views toolbar.

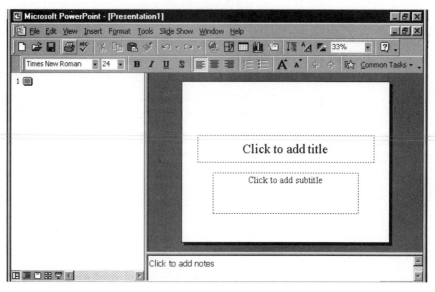

4. Your Title Slide should now be displayed in Slide view. PowerPoint is an incredibly intuitive and user-friendly program. You can learn a great deal about it just by following the on-screen instructions.

5. Click in the placeholder that says, "Click to add title." Type the text, "Mountain Bike Adventures".

6. Click in the placeholder that says, "Click to add subtitle." Type the text, "Riding in Washington State".

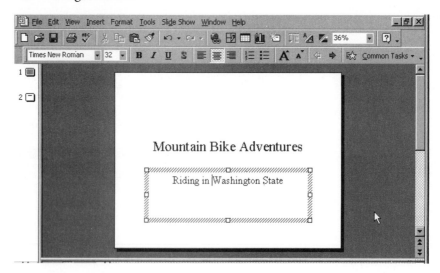

Save Your Presentation

1. From the Menu bar located at the top of the PowerPoint screen, choose File> Save As.

2. In the Save In: drop-down list box, navigate to your **Work in Progress** folder where you are saving your files. The Save as type: should be set to Presentation.

The first time you save a presentation before you have given it a name, you can also access the Save As dialog box by choosing File>Save or Control-S.

3. In the File name: text box at the bottom of the screen, type "Mountain Bike Adventures".

4. Click Save.

Add Slides to Your Presentation

1. From the Common Tasks drop-down menu located at the right side of the Formatting toolbar, choose New Slide.

You can also add a new slide by clicking on the New Slide button on the Standard Toolbar or use the keyboard shortcut, Control-M.

2. The New Slide dialog box displays a list of the available AutoLayouts for your slide. Choose Bulleted List and click OK.

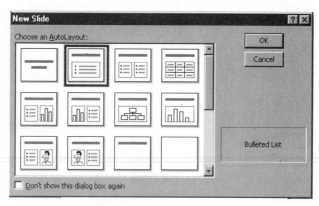

Once you save the presentation with a name, choosing File>Save or Control-S will automatically overwrite the existing file with the latest version of the file. In other words, these options will perform a quick save, but will not allow you to save the file under a different file name.

3. Click in the placeholder that says, "Click to add title." Type the text, "Pedal where the pavement ends".

4. Click in the placeholder that says, "Click to add text." Type the text, "Olympic Mountains", then press Enter.

5. A new bullet will automatically appear. Type the text, "North Cascades", press Enter, type "South Cascades" press Enter, and type "Puget Sound". Your slide should look like the one below.

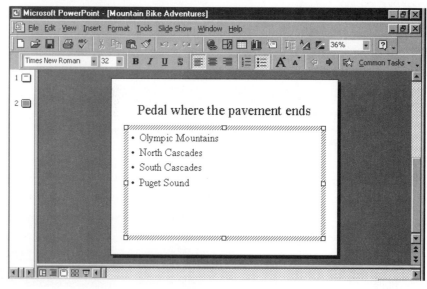

6. Click the Save button on the Standard toolbar to save your presentation.

7. Repeat Steps 1-5 above to add the following slides. Choose the 2 Column Text slide layout for Slide 4, Equipment.

Trail Rating

- Easy
- Moderate
- Skilled
- Adventurous

Equipment

• Bike	• Toe-Clips
• Helmet	• Cycle Computer
• Glasses	• Bike Bag or Pack
• Gloves	• Tire Repair Kit
• Clothing	• Bicycle Repair Kit
• Shoes	• First-Aid Kit

A Note About Safety

- Be knowledgeable
- Be prepared
- Be alert

8. Click Save.

9. Close the Mountain Bike Adventures presentation by choosing File>Close from the Menu bar. If you are asked to save changes, choose Yes.

PowerPoint Views

As mentioned earlier, there are different ways to view your PowerPoint presentation. Each view serves a slightly different purpose and each is useful depending upon what you are trying to accomplish. You can switch views by clicking on the appropriate view button on the View toolbar. The current view will be displayed in the status bar at the bottom of the screen. In addition, the button or icon of the current view

When you close the Mountain Bike Adventures file your screen will appear with a gray background and many of the commands will be disabled until you start a new presentation or open an existing one.

appears to be depressed or pushed in. You can also switch views by choosing the appropriate view from the View command on the Menu bar. The descriptions below should help you determine when you might want to switch views.

Slide View

Slide view displays each individual slide. If you wish to create or edit a presentation and see each slide as it will appear in your presentation, Slide view is an excellent choice. While you are working in Slide view you may insert text, graphs, charts, clip art, diagrams, and other elements. In this view, the Drawing toolbar will automatically appear at the bottom of the screen. This toolbar can be used to create and modify drawing objects that can enhance the effectiveness of your presentation.

Outline View

Many people are accustomed to preparing a presentation from an outline. To do so in PowerPoint, you can use Outline view. This view is perhaps the fastest way to enter all of the text for a presentation. In addition, it provides an excellent view of the overall presentation and can be most effective for developing the content. In addition, in Outline view you can quickly organize and reorganize your content by changing the order of the bullets or slides.

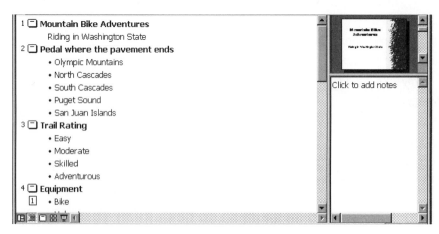

You can change the view of your PowerPoint presentation using a variety of different views available from the Views toolbar.

Slide Sorter View

Slide Sorter view displays a miniature of each slide and displays all of the slides at once. This view is most useful when you need to change the order of the slides in your presentation. In addition, you can cut and copy slides from your presentation from this view. Some special effects, such as transitions, can be applied while in this view.

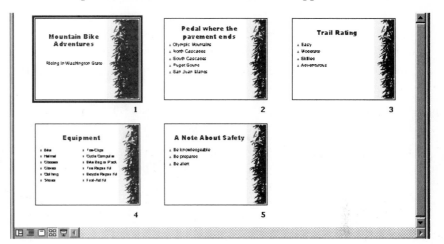

Normal View

Normal view is new to PowerPoint 2000. In addition to preparing the presentation that your audience will see, you may also wish to prepare speaker's notes for yourself or the presenter. You can do this in Normal view. This view provides a reduced image of the slide with an area below the slide image where you can add notes or text. This view combines Slide, Outline, and Notes Page views, giving you the ability to see your presentation in all of these views at the same time.

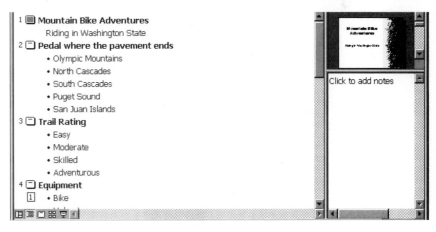

Slide Show View

Slide Show view is used to present your presentation electronically. In this view, each slide fills the computer screen and the effects of transitions, animation, and slide timings are displayed. To get out of this view, press Esc or keep clicking the left mouse button until you have viewed the entire presentation.

Open a Presentation and Navigate Among Different Views

1. Click File>Open from the Menu bar.

2. Navigate to your **Work in Progress** folder, select the **Mountain Bike Adventures** file, and choose Open.

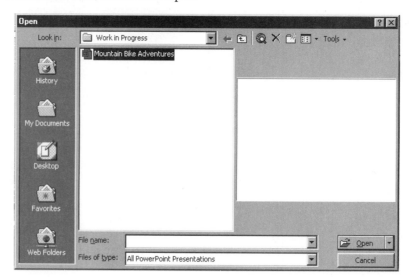

3. From the Views toolbar in the bottom left-hand corner of your screen, click on the first View button, Normal view. Your slide should appear as shown. In this view, you'll see the outline to the left, the slide at the right, and the notes area at the bottom.

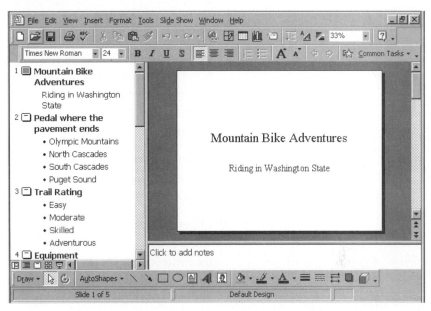

4. In the Outline section in the left pane, click at the end of Puget Sound and press Enter to add a fifth bullet. Type the text, "San Juan Islands". As you type this text, you'll see the text appear in both the outline and on the slide in the right pane.

5. Click on the Outline View button and you'll see that the left pane containing the outline is enlarged.

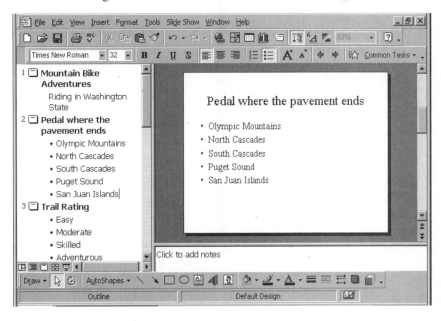

6. Click on the Slide View button. In Slide view, the left pane shrinks and the right pane is enlarged to display more of the slide.

In any of these first three views, you can move from one slide to the next by either clicking on the slide number in Outline view or using the Vertical Scroll bar at the right of the screen. Using the Up and Down arrows at the top and bottom of this scroll bar will allow you to move from slide to slide. In addition, you can use the Double-Up and Double-Down arrows at the bottom of the Scroll bar to move from slide to slide. Drag the Scroll box, and a tool tip will appear identifying the slide number and title of the slide that will be active if you release the left mouse button at that point. Try each of these methods of moving from slide to slide in your presentation.

7. Click the Slide Sorter button. In this view, you'll see a miniature version of many or all of the slides in the presentation. In this view you can delete slides, rearrange slides, or add transitions and animation to slides.

8. Click the last view button, Slide Show view. This view is used to display your on-screen presentation. In this view your toolbars disappear and your slides take up the entire screen. To advance from one slide to the next, click the left mouse button or press the Right Arrow key on your keyboard. To return to the previous slide, press the Left Arrow key or click the right mouse button and choose previous.

Mountain Bike Adventures

Riding in Washington State

9. Advance to the last slide of your presentation and click the mouse a final time.

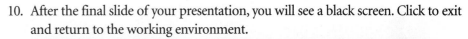

10. After the final slide of your presentation, you will see a black screen. Click to exit and return to the working environment.

End of slide show, click to exit.

11. Click Save.

12. Leave the file open.

Design Templates

A design template is a preset format that includes the colors and appearance of the background, as well as the type style of the titles, subtitles, and other text included in your presentation. It is very easy to apply a design template or to choose a different design template any time you wish to change the appearance of your presentation.

When you choose a design template, you will notice that the template is applied to every slide in your presentation. Though people who lack a background in design are often tempted to use a different background color and typeface on each slide, using a consistent design on all of the slides in your presentation will help you create a unified and harmonious presentation.

Applying a Design Template

1. With the file still open, switch to Normal view and go to Slide 1.

2. From the Common Tasks drop-down menu located at the right side of the Formatting toolbar, choose Apply Design Template.

You can also apply a design template by choosing Format>Apply Design from the Menu bar, or by right-clicking anywhere on the slide except on the border of a placeholder, and choose Apply Design.

If you do not see a preview on the right, make certain that the Preview button on the toolbar is depressed.

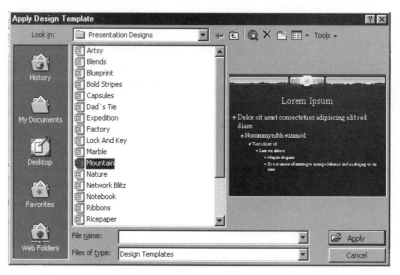

If the Mountain design template does not appear in your list of available presentation designs, choose a different template.

3. The Apply Design dialog box displays a list of the available design templates that you can select for your presentation. To see a preview of each design template before you apply it to your presentation, click on the design template name on the left and a preview will appear at the right.

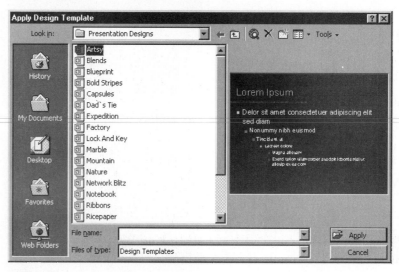

4. Click on the Mountain design template and choose Apply. Your presentation should now be formatted with the color, background, and fonts associated with the Mountain design template.

5. Go to the first slide in your presentation and click the last view button, Slide Show view on the Views toolbar . Continue clicking the left mouse button to preview the entire slide show with the design template that you just applied.

6. When you have returned to Normal View, save your presentation.

7. Close PowerPoint.

The AutoContent Wizard

In PowerPoint, you can use wizards to help you quickly create an effective presentation. Wizards guide you step by step and prompt you to respond to a series of questions. After you have responded to this series of questions, the structure and style of your presentation are complete. The final step is to insert the specific content.

The AutoContent Wizard is particularly helpful to those people who don't have a strong background in creating effective outlines for a presentation. The AutoContent Wizard allows you to choose the type of presentation from a list of categories such as "Recommending a Strategy," "Reporting Progress," or "Business Plan." Once you select a presentation category, the AutoContent Wizard will create an outline that you can follow. Though you probably won't find a category for every potential type of presentation you may need to create, the AutoContent Wizard is an excellent place to start because it does prepare a title slide and outline for you to edit. This not only saves you time, it also helps you generate ideas for topics that you should consider addressing in your presentation.

Create a Presentation Using the AutoContent Wizard

1. Start the PowerPoint application.

2. At the first PowerPoint dialog box, click the "AutoContent Wizard" radio button and choose OK.

You can also access the AutoContent Wizard by choosing File>New. Click on the Presentations tab>AutoContent Wizard>OK.

3. The first AutoContent Wizard dialog box should appear on your screen. Read the information in the dialog box and then click the Next button at the bottom of the dialog box to advance to the second dialog box, Presentation type.

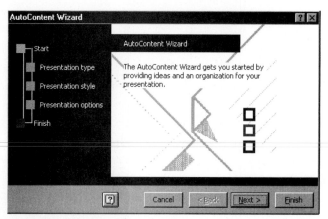

4. This second dialog box allows you to select the type of presentation. Click on the Sales/Marketing button and then click Selling a Product or Service. Choose Next.

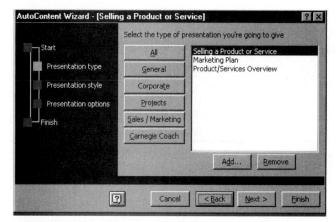

5. The third dialog box requests that you specify the type of output. The top radio button, "On-screen presentation" should be selected. Choose Next.

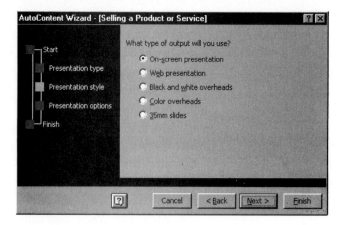

6. From the fourth dialog box you'll specify the title of the presentation as well as any information that you might want included in the footer at the bottom of each slide. In the Presentation title text box, type "Digital Cameras". Leave the Footer text box blank, but do leave check marks in the "Date last updated" and "Slide number" checkboxes. Choose Next.

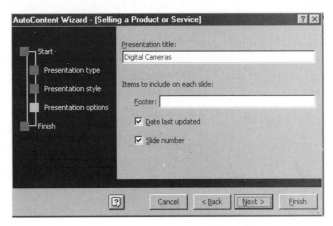

7. At the last step, choose Finish. PowerPoint displays the presentation you just created with the AutoContent Wizard in Normal view. You are now ready to modify the generic outline by adding the content specific to your presentation on digital cameras.

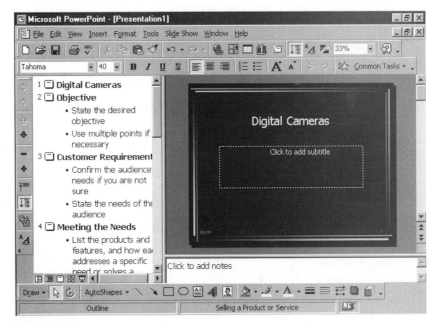

8. Leave the file open for the next exercise.

If a different design template appears on your slide, continue as instructed.

Modifying an Outline

In Normal view, you will notice that the AutoContent Wizard displays the outline with the title on Slide 1. This is the title slide. In addition to the title slide, you'll see seven additional slides with suggestions regarding the type of text that should be included on each of these slides.

It is now time to adapt the generic outline to your presentation by adding content specific to digital cameras. The AutoContent Wizard should be used as a guide. Don't feel that you are locked into the slides as they currently exist. Modify them as necessary to best meet your needs. To modify the outline, select or highlight the text in the placeholders and replace the existing text with your own text. You can also delete existing content if you feel that it doesn't apply to this particular presentation.

Modifying an Outline Created from the AutoContent Wizard

1. In the outline on the left, select the text "State the desired objective" under Objective on Slide 2. To select the text either click and drag across the existing text or position the four-headed arrow on the bullet to the left of the text and click. Once the text has been selected, type "Everyone should own a digital camera".

2. Select the text "Use multiple points if necessary" in the second bullet, and press the Delete or Backspace key to remove this item.

3. Select the text "Customer Requirements" in Slide 3.

If you can't see all of the text in the outline, you can resize the outline pane. To do so, position the mouse pointer on the border between the outline pane and the slide pane. The mouse will change to a double-headed arrow. Click and drag the mouse to the right to enlarge the outline pane.

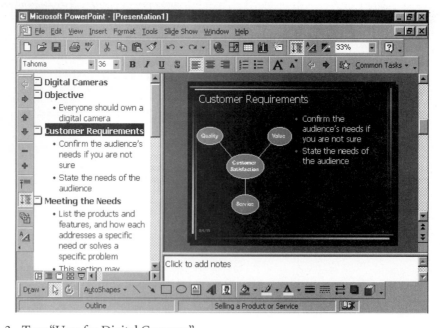

3. Type "Uses for Digital Cameras".

4. Click on each of the objects at the left of the slide to select the object as shown.

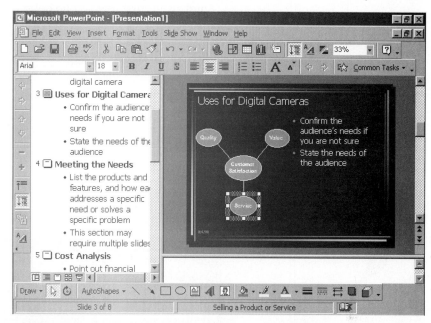

5. Press the Delete key to remove the objects from the slide.

If the object is not removed when you press the Delete key, click on the border of the object and try pressing Delete again or drag a marquee around the object to select all of it and press the Delete key.

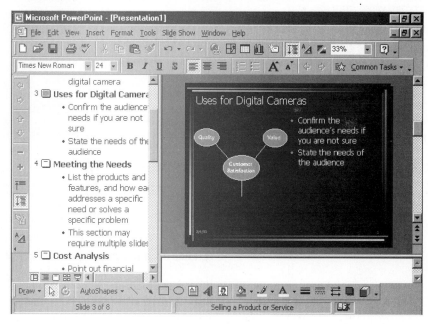

6. Repeat steps 4 and 5 to remove all of the objects except the Title and Text Placeholders from the slide.

7. Click on the Common Tasks drop-down list box and choose the Bulleted List AutoLayout (first row, second option). Click Apply.

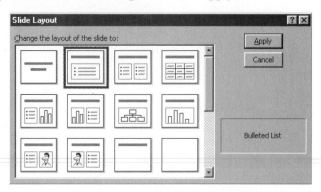

8. Finish typing the bulleted items on Slide 3 so that it appears as shown.

Though you can switch to most of the other PowerPoint views from the View command on the Menu bar, Outline view is not available from View on the Menu bar.

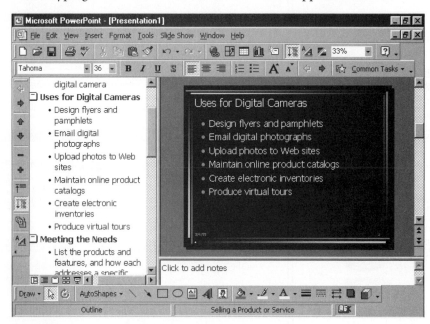

9. In the outline on the left, select the text "Meeting the Needs", which is the title for Slide 4. To select the text, click and drag across the existing text. Once the text has been selected, type "Benefits of Digital Cameras".

10. Repeat steps 6 and 7 to remove all of the objects except the Title and Text Placeholders, and change the slide layout.

11. Use the outline to finish Slide 4 so that it appears as shown below.

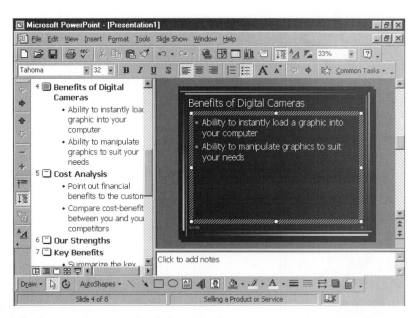

12. Switch to Outline view by clicking on the Outline View button on the Views toolbar.

13. Double-click on "Analysis" in Slide 5 to select it. Press Delete to delete the word.

14. Modify the text in Slide 5 so that it appears as shown.

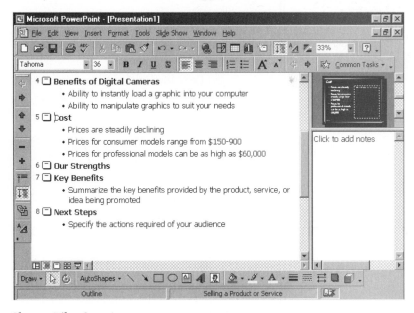

15. Choose File>Save As.

16. At the Save As dialog box, navigate to your **Work in Progress** folder.

17. Save your presentation as "Digital Cameras" and make certain that the Save As Type option is set to Presentation. Click Save and keep the file open.

Deleting Slides

1. In Outline view, position the mouse on the Slide icon next to Slide 6. When the mouse changes to a four-headed arrow, click to select the content of Slide 6.

2. Hold down the Shift key and click on the slide icon next to Slide 8 to select Slides 6-8.

If you make a mistake and delete the wrong slides, choose Edit>Undo Clear.

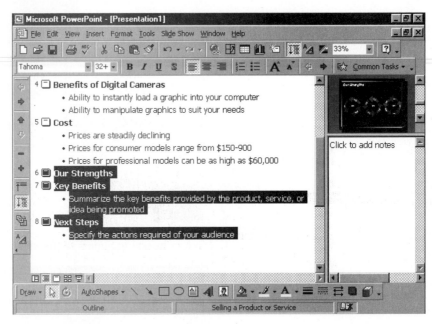

3. Press the Delete key to delete all three slides at once. A Warning will appear telling you that "This will delete a slide and its notes page along with any graphics. Do you want to continue?" Click OK.

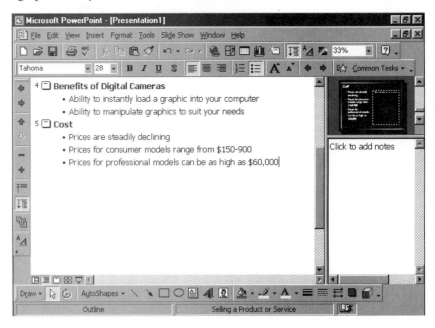

As you can see, it is quite easy to delete slides in Outline view. You can delete slides from several different views in PowerPoint. Next, you'll delete slides in Slide Sorter view.

4. Choose Edit>Undo Clear from the Menu bar. The three slides that you just deleted should reappear.

5. Click on the Slide Sorter View button to switch views.

6. Click on Slide 6. A dark border should appear around Slide 6. This border indicates the active or selected slide.

7. Hold down the Shift key and click on Slide 8. Slides 6, 7, and 8 should now appear with a darker border as shown below.

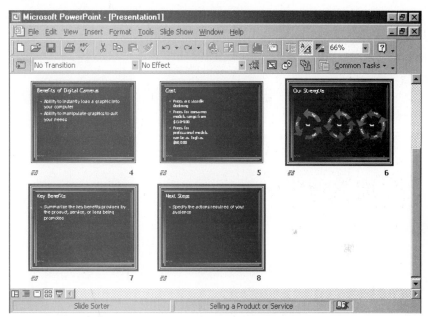

You can also switch to Slide Sorter view by choosing View>Slide Sorter from the Menu bar.

8. Press the Delete key to delete all three slides at one time.

9. Save your presentation.

10. Click on Slide 1 and switch to Slide Show view to preview all of the slides in your presentation.

11. Close your presentation and exit PowerPoint.

Complete Project A: The Backcountry Almanac

Notes:

CHAPTER 3

MODIFYING A PRESENTATION

CHAPTER OBJECTIVE:

To learn how to modify an existing presentation, while understanding the reasons why you may wish to so. In Chapter 3 you will:

- Learn to add text to an existing PowerPoint presentation.

- Learn to find and replace text in your presentation.

- Understand how to delete and add slides to your existing presentation.

- Learn how to copy slides from another presentation.

- Understand how to insert headers and footers into your presentation.

- Become familiar with the means to modify the Title and Slide Master for each presentation.

- Learn to reorder slides in Slide Sorter View.

- Learn how to modify the sequence of slides in Outline or Normal View.

- Become familiar with applying a new design template.

PROJECTS TO BE COMPLETED:

- The Backcountry Almanac
- **Fitness Facts**
- Mastering Golf
- Easy & Elegant Baking
- Wildflower Spas
- Washington Apples Online
- Yard Debris Recycling Program

Modifying a Presentation

In Chapter 2 you learned how to create a new slide show from a blank presentation or from the AutoContent Wizard. In this chapter, you will learn how to modify an existing presentation. There are many reasons why you may wish to modify your presentation. For example, you may wish to delete a slide or change the order of existing slides. You may need to change the text on a slide or slides. You may also want to use a different slide layout or design template. You can further customize your presentation by using the Slide and Title Masters as well as headers and footers.

You have been asked to update a PowerPoint presentation on Buying a Personal Computer. Many of the specifications in this presentation are outdated. Consequently, you will need to replace much of the existing content. In addition, you will need to add some text, rearrange and delete some slides, modify the slide masters, and add headers and footers.

Open an Existing Presentation

1. Start PowerPoint. From the **SF-PowerPoint** folder, open the **Buying a PC** file.

2. Display Slide 1 of the presentation.

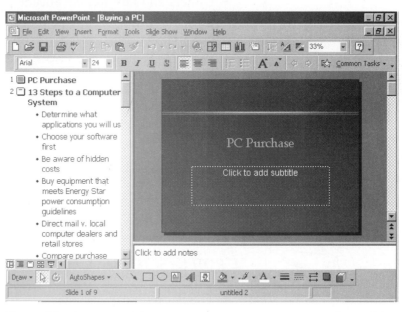

3. Choose File>Save As. Navigate to your **Work in Progress** and save this presentation as "Buying a PC – Updated".

4. Leave this presentation open for the next exercise.

You can modify text in an existing presentation by selecting the text and replacing it with new text. In this next session you will change existing text and add new text to a presentation.

Modifying and Adding Text

1. Select the title "PC Purchase" by clicking and dragging across the text.

2. Type "Buying a Personal Computer" to change the title.

3. Click in the placeholder that reads "Click to add subtitle." Type your name.

4. Leave the presentation open for the next exercise.

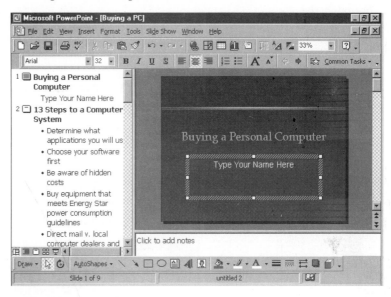

Find and Replace

If you need to locate a word or phrase in your PowerPoint presentation, you can have PowerPoint find the word or phrase for you through the use of the Find feature. In addition to finding text or manually searching for text and then selecting it and replacing it with new text, you may also wish to use the Find and Replace feature. Find and Replace commands are helpful when you have a long presentation and cannot find what you are searching for. In addition, Find and Replace provides greater assurance that you have replaced all occurrences of a word or phrase.

The Find and Replace dialog box may hide the text in the slide. Move the Find and Replace dialog box by dragging the blue title bar.

Some additional options at the Find and Replace dialog box include Match Case and Find Whole Words Only. When you check the Match Case checkbox, PowerPoint requires a case-sensitive match for uppercase and lowercase letters. Find Whole Words Only requires spaces or punctuation on either side of the word so that the search string won't be located within another word. For example, if you type in "the" in the Find What text box, checking Find Whole Words Only will prevent "the" from being found in "ano*the*r" or "mo*the*r" or "*the*se."

Using Find and Replace to Modify a Presentation

1. Click Edit on the Menu bar.

2. Choose Replace.

3. Type "486DX2" in the Find what: text box.

4. Type "Pentium III" in the Replace with: text box.

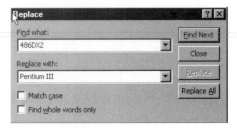

You may need to point to the double chevrons at the bottom of the menu before you see the Replace command.

5. Click the Find Next button to locate the first occurrence of "486DX2."

6. Click Replace. You should see that "486DX2" is replaced with Pentium III on Slide 4 of the presentation, and a message appears on your screen to notify you that PowerPoint has finished searching your presentation and that no more occurrences of "486DX2" were found. If PowerPoint had found additional occurrences of "486DX2" it would have highlighted each occurrence giving you the option to replace the text. In addition, you could use the "Replace All" command button which tells PowerPoint to conduct a global Find and Replace without prompting you to verify the replacement of each occurrence.

Control-H is the keyboard shortcut for Replace. You can also use Find to locate text and other elements of a PowerPoint presentation. The keyboard shortcut for Find is Control-F.

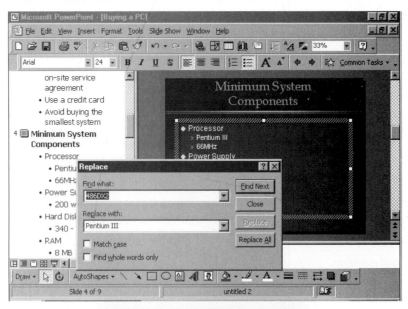

7. Click OK to close this dialog box.

8. Click on the "x" in the upper right-hand corner of the Find and Replace dialog box to close this dialog box.

Many times when you are using PowerPoint you will be presenting from either a bulleted or numbered list. You should use a numbered list if the order of the steps is important or if the items on the list are being counted. Otherwise, use a bulleted list.

Change Bullets to Numbers

1. Display Slide 2 of the presentation. Because the title of this slide is "13 Steps to a Computer System," a numbered list would probably be a better option than a bulleted list.

2. Select the six-bulleted items in Slide 2.

3. Click Format on the Menu bar.

4. Choose Bullets and Numbering.

5. At the Bullets and Numbering dialog box, click on the Numbered tab.

6. Click on the first option, Arabic numerals followed by a period. Click OK.

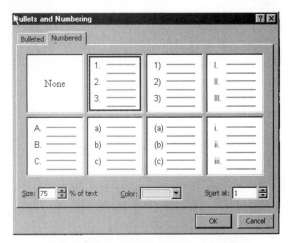

The bulleted list will appear as shown in the following image.

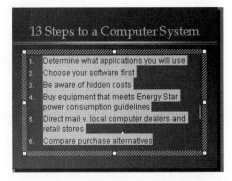

When you open the Find or Find and Replace dialog box, the previous search string will be displayed. To remove it before performing another search, select the text and press Delete or type in the new search string.

7. Display Slide 3.

8. Select the seven bulleted items in Slide 3.

9. Repeat steps 3-5 above.

10. From the Bullets and Numbering dialog box, click on the second option, Arabic numerals followed by a period. Change the Start at: spin box in the lower right-hand corner of the dialog box to 7. Click OK.

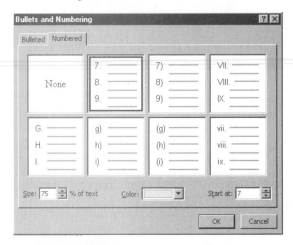

The bulleted list will appear as shown.

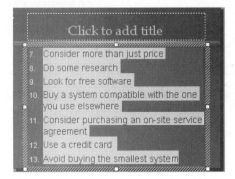

Modifying and Deleting Text

1. With the same presentation still open, change the text on Slide 4 as shown.

2. Display Slide 6.

3. Position the mouse pointer to the left of "5.25 inch" in the Outline.

4. When the mouse pointer changes to a crosshair or four-headed arrow, click to select "5.25 inch."

5. Press the Delete key to delete this bullet.

6. Change "14 or 15" to "17 to 21" as shown.

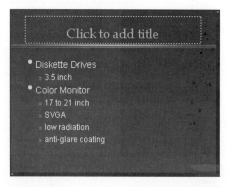

7. Modify Slides 7-9 as they appear below. Don't forget to delete the title on Slide 9. To do so, select the text and press the Delete key.

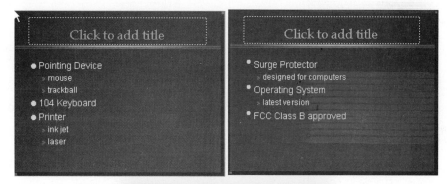

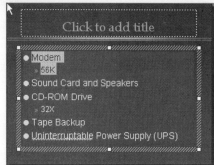

8. Save this modified PowerPoint Presentation and keep it open.

At times, you may need to combine several presentations into one, or copy slides from one presentation into another. Rather than retyping the slide in the presentation, you can insert a slide or slides from one presentation into another presentation.

Copying a Slide From Another Presentation

1. Display Slide 9, which is the final slide of the presentation. When you insert a slide from another presentation you should first display the slide that will precede the slide to be inserted. In this case, the inserted slide will become the final slide of the presentation.

2. Click Insert>Slides from Files on the Menu bar.

3. At the Slide Finder dialog box, click on the Find Presentation tab.

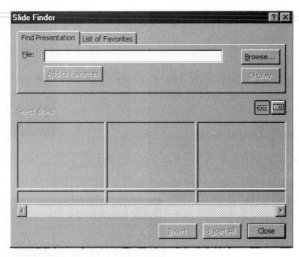

If you wish to insert more than one slide from a presentation, at the Slide Finder dialog box, click on each slide to be inserted or choose Insert All to select and insert all of the slides from the presentation.

4. Click Browse, and locate the presentation titled "Company Information."

5. Select "Company Information," and choose Open.

6. Click Display.

7. Select Slide 1 from the grid at the bottom of the dialog box.

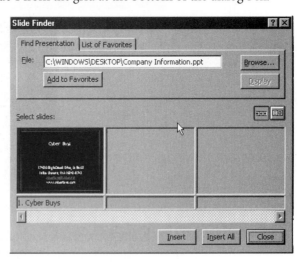

8. Click Insert.

9. Close the Slide Finder dialog box.

If the Master toolbar does not appear, choose View>Toolbars>Master.

You are not limited to the font sizes from the drop-down menu. To change the font size to a size other than those listed in the drop-down list box, select the existing font size in the text box and type in the new font size.

10. The Cyber Buys company information slide becomes Slide 10. Notice that the formatting from the existing design template is applied to the slide that has been inserted or copied from another presentation.

11. Save the presentation and keep it open for the next few exercises.

Title and Slide Masters

There are two different masters for each slide presentation — the Title Master and the Slide Master. The Title Master controls the look of the title slide and the Slide Master controls the look of the remaining slides in the presentation. Every presentation has masters that control the appearance and layout of the slides in a presentation. Although the design template determines what the slides will look like, you can modify or override the appearance of the design template by modifying the Title and Slide Masters. A change to the Title Master will modify the title slide while a change to the Slide Master will modify all of the remaining slides in the presentation.

Some of the components of the Title and Slide Master that you might consider modifying include the font, font size, font style, alignment, color scheme, background graphics, logos, drawn objects, bullets, slide number, date, time, and line spacing. Although you could make changes to these components on each individual slide, by modifying the Slide Master, the change is applied to all of the slides at one time. This can save you a considerable amount of time.

Modifying Title and Slide Masters

1. Display Slide 1.

2. Click on View>Master>Slide Master from the Menu bar.

3. Click on the placeholder that says "Click to edit Master title style" and change the font size to 42 pts.

4. Click View>Normal or choose Close from the Master toolbar.

5. Click anywhere in the title text of Slide 1 and check the Font Size box. It should read 42.

6. Click anywhere in the title text of Slide 4 and check the Font Size box. It should also read 42. As you can see, modifying the Slide Master allows you to modify all of the slides in the presentation at once.

Inserting Headers and Footers

Information that appears at the top of every page or slide is called a header. Information that appears at the bottom of every page or slide is called a footer. Common information appearing in headers and footers includes the date, page or slide number, presentation title, and name of the presenter. Like Title and Slide Master, headers and footers keep you from having to add the same information (dates, page numbers, etc.) on each page or slide. Instead, you add this information to the header or footer one time and it appears on every page or every slide in the presentation.

Often, a printout of a presentation outline is provided to the audience as handouts. Descriptive headers and footers can be added to these audience handouts to help provide identifying information about the printed items.

In the next steps, you'll add headers and footers to both the online presentation and audience handouts for the Buying a Personal Computer presentation.

Inserting Headers and Footers

1. Display Slide 1.

2. Choose View>Header and Footer from the Menu bar.

3. At the Header and Footer dialog box, click the Slide tab.

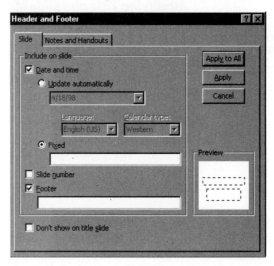

4. If necessary, add a check mark next to Date and time and select the radio button Fixed. In the Fixed text box, type in December 3, 2000.

5. If necessary, add a check mark next to Slide number and Footer.

6. Enter the text, "Buying a Personal Computer" into the Footer text box.

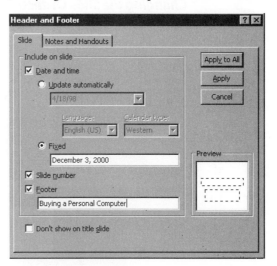

7. Click on the Notes and Handouts tab.

8. Repeat steps 4-6, and make certain that there is a check mark next to the Page number checkbox in the Header and Footer dialog box.

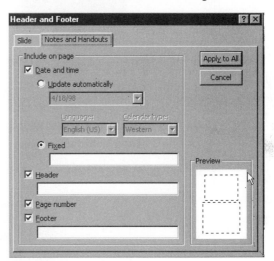

9. Choose Apply to All.

10. Save the Presentation.

Rearranging Slides

Rearranging the order of slides in a presentation is a common task. Perhaps one of the easiest ways to change the order of the slides in a presentation is to use Slide Sorter view. In Slide Sorter view you'll see a miniature of each slide in the presentation. This view enables you to see many of the slides at one time. Consequently, it is easy to rearrange the order of the slides by moving them around using drag and drop.

Changing the Slide Order using Slide Sorter View

1. Display Slide 1.

2. Click the Slide Sorter View button on the Views toolbar or choose View>Slide Sorter to switch to Slide Sorter view.

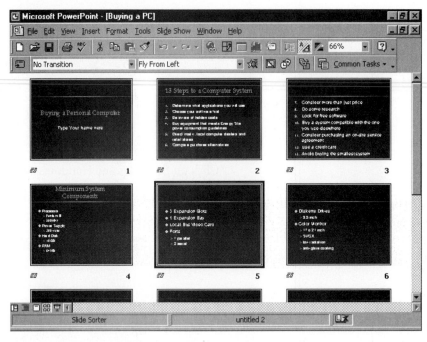

In addition to moving a slide in Slide Sorter view, you can also copy a slide. To do so, hold down the Control key and drag the slide (vertical line) to its new location. When you release the left mouse button, a duplicate slide will appear.

3. Click on Slide 6 and drag the slide to the left. As you drag the mouse pointer, a vertical line will appear.

4. Position the vertical line to the left of Slide 5 and release the left mouse button.

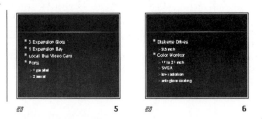

Slides 5 and 6 should now be reordered and renumbered.

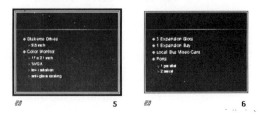

5. Save the presentation.

Changing the Slide Order using Outline View

In addition to changing the slide order in Slide Sorter view, you can also change the order or sequence of the slides in a presentation from Outline view.

1. Display Slide 1.

2. Click the Outline View button on the Views toolbar to switch to Outline view.

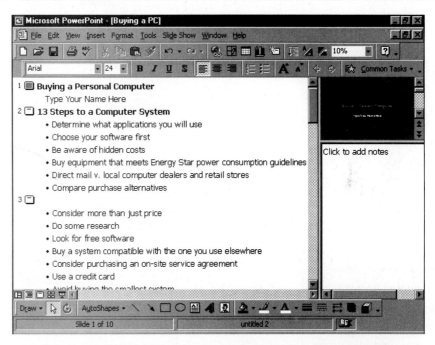

3. Scroll down until both Slides 5 and 6 can be viewed at the same time.

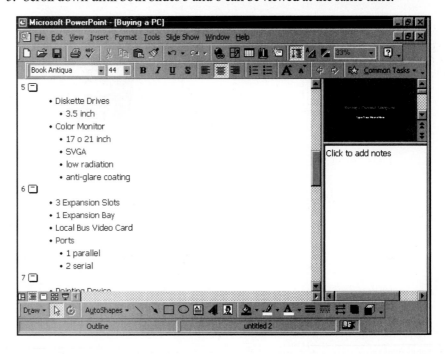

4. Point to the Slide icon adjacent to Slide 5.

5. When the mouse pointer appears as a four-headed arrow or crosshair, click the left mouse button. All of the text levels in Slide 5 should now be selected.

Another way to rearrange slides in Outline view is to use the Move Up or Move Down buttons from the Outlining toolbar.

6. Drag the slide down in the outline.

7. Position the horizontal line that appears on your screen below all of the text in Slide 6 and release the left mouse button. Slides 5 and 6 should now be reordered.

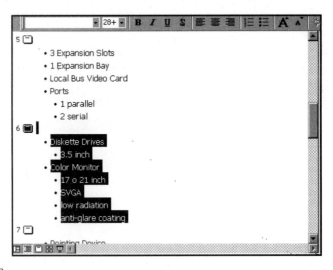

8. Click Save.

A light bulb on your slide indicates that a tip is available from the Office Assistant. Click on the light bulb to read the tip and then close the Office Assistant to continue.

Changing the Slide Layout

Slides can be added to a presentation by using one of the predefined slide formats or AutoLayouts available in PowerPoint. In addition, you can change the existing layout of a slide at any time. Though you can change the slide layout from Outline view, we are going to switch to Slide view so that the change in layout is obvious.

1. Click anywhere on Slide 10, the last slide in the presentation, to make it the active slide.

2. Click on the Slide View button on the Views toolbar to switch to Slide view.

3. From the Common Tasks drop-down menu on the Formatting toolbar, choose Slide Layout.

4. From the Slide Layout dialog box, click on the Text & Clip Art AutoLayout (first option in the third row) and choose Reapply.

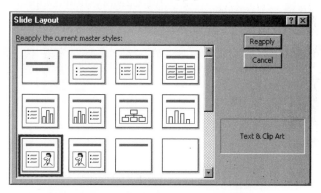

The Text & Clip Art layout is now applied to Slide 10.

5. Double-click the placeholder that reads, "Double-click to add clip art." The Microsoft Clip Gallery should appear.

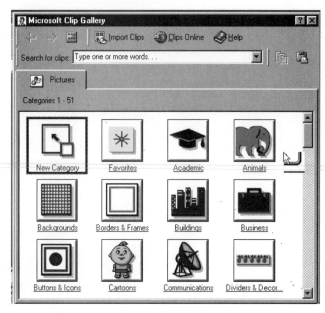

If you cannot find the clip art image used in these instructions, choose a different, but appropriate clip art.

6. Scroll down and click on the "Science & Tech..." category. A list of clip art from this category should appear on your screen.

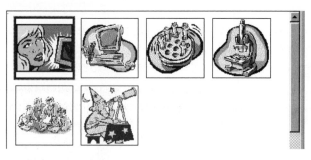

7. Click on the clip art image of the computer (second option in the first row) and from the available callout options that appear, choose Insert Clip.

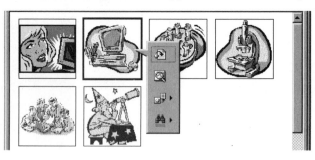

The clip art image of the computer should now appear on Slide 10.

8. Save your presentation.

Scale and Size Objects and Placeholders

It is often necessary to resize objects and placeholders that appear on your slide so that you can customize the position and size of the media elements included on your slides.

1. Click once on the clip art image. The Picture toolbar will appear on your screen and you should see small white boxes appear around the clip art image. These small white boxes are called selection or sizing handles.

If you don't see the Picture toolbar on your screen, choose View>Toolbars> Picture.

2. Click on the Close button in the upper-right corner of the Picture toolbar to remove this toolbar from your screen. You'll learn more about the Picture toolbar in a later chapter.

3. Position your mouse pointer on top of the sizing handle in the lower right-hand corner of the clip art image until the mouse changes to a double-headed arrow.

4. Drag the lower-right sizing handle up and to the left. As you drag, you'll notice that the clip art image becomes smaller.

5. Keep dragging until the clip art image is approximately the same size as the computer shown in the slide below or about one-quarter of its original size.

6. Save your presentation.

Move Objects and Placeholders

1. Click anywhere in the Title Placeholder that reads "Cyber Buys." Sizing handles appear around the placeholder for the title.

2. Position the mouse pointer on top of the middle-right sizing handle until the mouse pointer changes to a double-headed arrow.

3. Click and drag to the left to resize the title placeholder as shown.

When the mouse pointer changes to a double-headed arrow, this usually indicates that an object or placeholder will be resized. When the mouse pointer changes to a four-headed arrow, this usually indicates that an object or place-holder will be moved.

4. Click once on the clip art image to select it.

5. Position the mouse pointer on top of the clip art image until the mouse pointer changes to a four-headed arrow.

6. Drag the clip art image to the upper right-hand corner of the slide as shown and resize the image as necessary to make the slide look well balanced.

7. Click anywhere on the bulleted list. Once again, you will see sizing handles appear around the placeholder for the bulleted list.

8. Position the mouse pointer on top of the middle-right sizing handle

9. When the mouse pointer changes to a double-headed arrow, click and drag to resize the placeholder as shown.

10. Click and drag the top middle sizing handle down to add space between the title and the address on Slide 10.

11. Select the four bulleted items and choose Format>Bullets and Numbering. From the Bullets and Numbering dialog box, choose None.

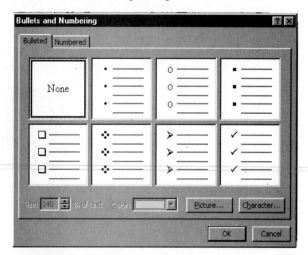

12. Click on the Center Alignment button  on the Formatting toolbar to center the text as shown.

13. Save your presentation.

14. Make Slide 1 active and switch to Slide Show view to preview your presentation.

Printing the Presentation

1. Choose File>Print from the Menu bar.

2. At the Print dialog box, set the Print Range to All.

3. From the Print what: drop-down list box, choose Handouts and set the Slides per page to 6.

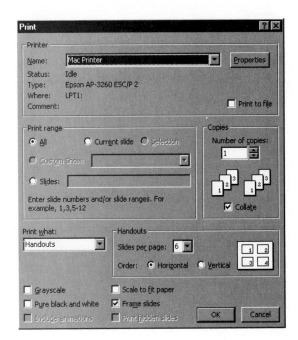

4. Click Print.

5. Close the document without saving changes.

6. Exit PowerPoint.

Complete Project B: Fitness Facts

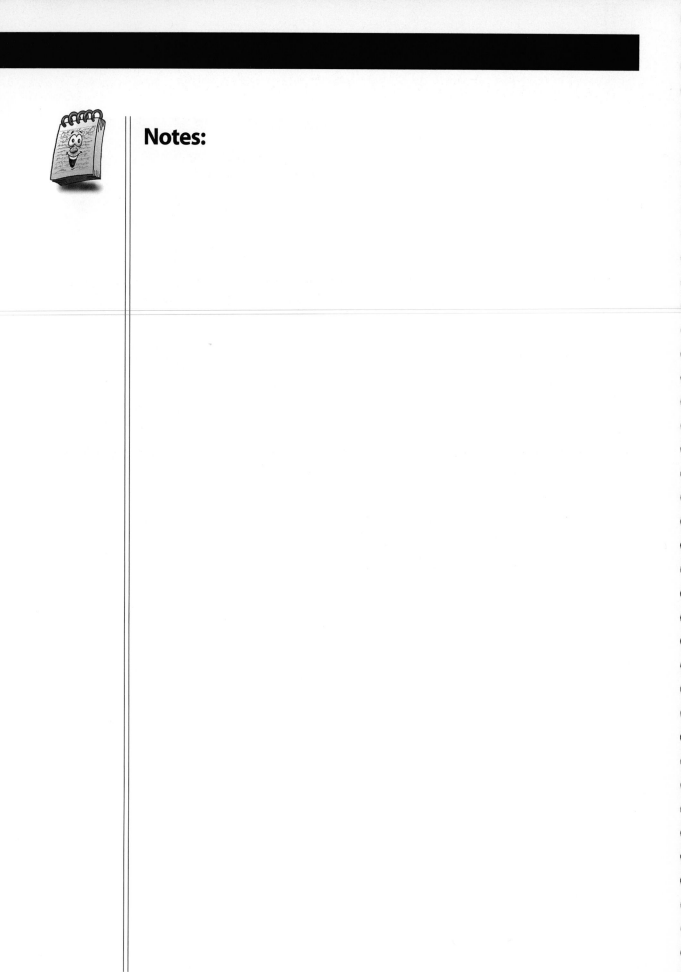

Notes:

CHAPTER 4

WORKING WITH TEXT

CHAPTER OBJECTIVE:

To learn the different methods for adding text to your PowerPoint presentation, and to understand how to add text to your presentation from almost any view. In Chapter 4 you will:

- Understand how to enter text in different views: in Outline view or to the placeholders designated in Slide view.

- Learn to add text outside of existing placeholders by creating a text box.

- Understand how to change fonts on all slides, as well as individual slides.

- Learn to use the Format Painter, which allows you to pick up formatting from the existing text and apply the same formatting to any other text in your presentation.

- Become familiar with the methods of changing the alignment of text in a text box.

- Learn the value of Undo and Redo.

- Learn how to promote and demote text.

- Become familiar with PowerPoint's WordArt application.

- Understand how to create text boxes.

- Learn how to check spelling.

PROJECTS TO BE COMPLETED:

- The Backcountry Almanac
- Fitness Facts
- **Mastering Golf**
- Easy & Elegant Baking
- Wildflower Spas
- Washington Apples Online
- Yard Debris Recycling Program

Working with Text

Entering Text in Different Views

There are several different methods for adding text to your PowerPoint presentation and you can add text to your presentation from almost any view. In addition to adding text to the presentation in Outline view or adding text to the placeholders designated in Slide view, there are also times when you may need to add text outside of the existing placeholders. You can do this by simply creating a text box.

Adding and Modifying Text

1. Start the PowerPoint application.

2. Select Open an existing presentation from the initial PowerPoint screen and click OK.

3. Click on the drop-down list box next to Look in: and navigate to the **SF-PowerPoint** folder. Open the file called **Ergonomics**.

4. If your presentation is not displaying in Normal view, switch views by clicking on the Normal View button on the Views toolbar or choose View>Normal view from the Menu bar.

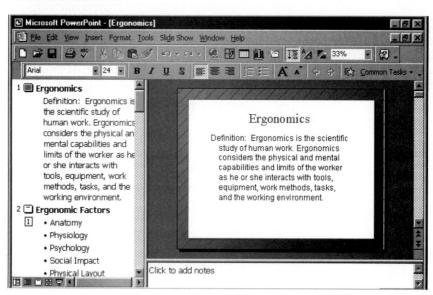

You can also open a presentation by double-clicking on the icon next to the file name.

5 Leave the presentation open.

Line Spacing

When you enter text in a PowerPoint text box, by default it will be single spaced. Rather than inserting hard returns in your slides to adjust the space between lines of text, it is often easier and more effective to adjust the line spacing. You can change the line spacing for a single slide or you can adjust the line spacing for all of the slides at once. The Line Spacing command is located under Format on the Menu bar. At the Line Spacing dialog box you will see that you have a the option to adjust the Line Spacing, the amount of space Before a paragraph, or the amount of space After a paragraph. The spacing is measured in either Lines or Points and the text must be selected before the Line Spacing feature is accessible.

In addition, if you wish to see a preview of the spacing changes you have set before they are actually applied to the slide, you can click the Preview button on the right-hand side of the dialog box.

When preparing slides for a presentation, you do not want to include too much information on each slide. In addition, for slides to be readable, you should have enough space between lines so that the text is easy for the audience to read. Think of each PowerPoint slide as a note to the audience. The slides are not meant to tell the story without help from the speaker. The speaker should discuss and add to each slide during the presentation.

Changing the Line Spacing on a Single Slide

1. Select and delete the text on Slide 1 so that it appears as shown. You will also need to add appropriate capitalization.

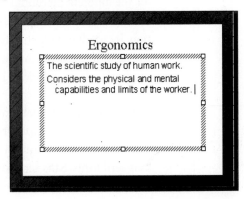

2. Position the mouse pointer on the upper-middle sizing handle. When the mouse pointer changes to a double-headed arrow, drag down to resize the text box so that it is centered on the screen.

3. Select all of the text in the lower placeholder.

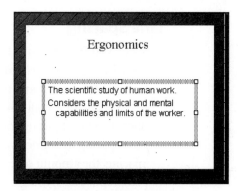

*When choosing between Points or Lines from the Spacing dialog box, keep in mind that a **line** is the current line height based on the selected font size while a **point** is a unit used to measure the vertical height of text. For comparison purposes, 72 points is equal to one inch. Points generally offer a wider range of spacing options than do lines.*

4. Choose Format>Line Spacing. At the Line Spacing dialog box, set the Before paragraph spacing to 1 line. Click OK.

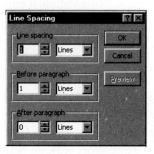

5. Save the presentation into your **Work in Progress** folder and name it "Ergonomics Updated". Leave this file open for the following exercises.

Modifying Slides

Though design templates are usually quite attractive and well thought out, you may find a need to modify a template. For example, you might like the background and color scheme used in a template, but not appreciate the fonts that have been selected for the different placeholders on each slide. Modifying each slide individually would be a time-consuming process, particularly if the presentation is quite large. In addition, by modifying each slide individually, you run the risk of failing to make a change to one or more slides. An easier way to modify all of the slides in the presentation is to modify the Master Slide as illustrated earlier in the book.

Serif fonts are fonts that have serifs or little lines on the end of each horizontal or vertical line. For example, from the list below, Book Antiqua, Bookman Old Style, Courier New, and Garamond would be examples of serif fonts. The other fonts are sans serif fonts. Sans serif fonts do not have serifs or little lines on the end of each horizontal and vertical line.

According to design principles, serif fonts are easier to read because the serifs or little lines help our eyes track text on the page. On the other hand, sans serif fonts have a more contemporary look and are more appropriate for titles and headings.

Changing the Font on all Slides

1. Switch to Slide Show view and view the entire presentation. When you have finished viewing the presentation, switch to Normal view and make Slide 1 active.

2. Choose View>Master>Slide Master.

3. Select the text that reads "Click to edit Master title style."

If the Master toolbar is on top of the Master slide, move it by dragging the blue Title bar.

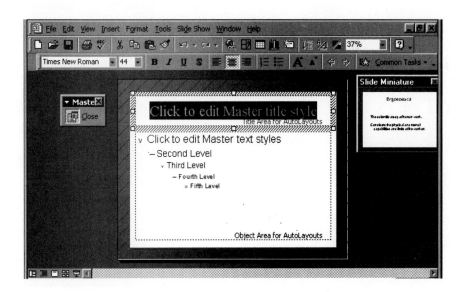

4. Choose Format>Font from the Menu bar.

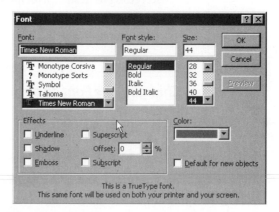

5. From the Font dialog box, click on Arial under Font to change the title font for all slides in the presentation from Times New Roman, a serif font, to Arial, a sans serif font. Click OK.

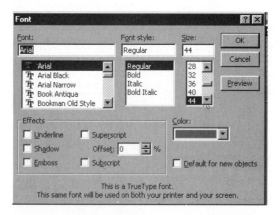

6. Select all of the text in the lower text placeholder. You should have selected the text from "Click to edit Master text styles" through "Fifth Level."

7. Choose Format>Font and change the font for the selected text to ATC Island. Click OK. Deselect the text by clicking outside of the selection.

Changing the Bullet Style on all Slides

In addition to changing the font style for each slide, you may wish to change other elements of the design template. Next we will customize the bullet that is used for the first level heading.

1. Click anywhere in the line of text that reads, "Click to edit Master text styles."

2. Choose Format>Bullets and Numbering.

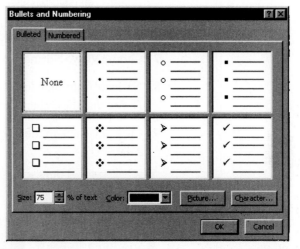

3. From the Bullets and Numbering dialog box, make certain that the Bulleted tab is selected and choose Character…in the lower right-hand corner.

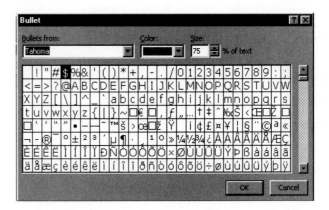

4. From the drop-down list box under Bullets from…, choose Tahoma.

5. Click on any symbol in the grid to see a larger preview of the symbol.

The Tahoma font ships with PowerPoint and should be installed on your system. If Tahoma is not available from the Bullets From: drop-down list box, choose a different option.

6. Choose the Chevrons (fifth row, last option) and click OK.

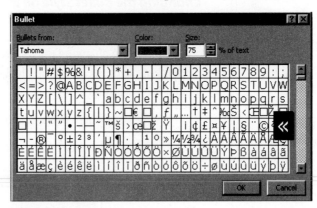

7 Choose View>Normal from the Menu bar.

8. Navigate from slide to slide to see the results of the change in font and bullet. Notice that these changes were applied to all of the slides in the presentation.

9. Click anywhere in the title placeholder of any slide. The font should be set to Arial.

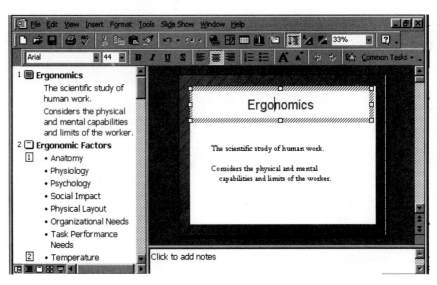

Due to the change of font, the appearance of the text on some of the slides may have been compromised.

10. Click anywhere in the text placeholder on any slide. The font should be set to Island, which is the font set on the Master slide.

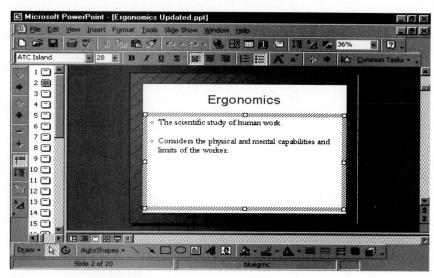

11. Save your presentation.

Modifying a Single Slide

At times, you may need to override the font or font style from the design template on a single slide only.

Changing the Font on a Single Slide

1. Switch to Slide view by clicking on the Slide View button on the Views toolbar.

2. Scroll to Slide 7, the title of this slide should read "Example."

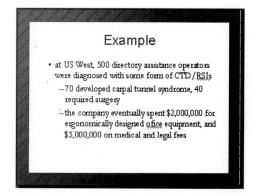

3. Select "$2,000,000" and choose Format>Font from the Menu bar.

4. From the Font dialog box, click on the drop-down list box under Color and choose dark green, the third option in the row under Automatic. This row of colors follows the color scheme that has been established in the design template.

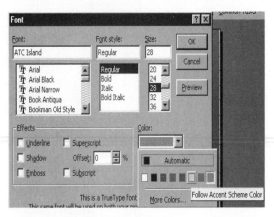

5. Change the Font style to Bold and the Font Size to 36. Click OK.

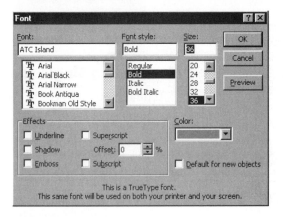

6. Save your presentation.

The Format Painter

The Format Painter is a wonderful tool. By allowing you to pick up formatting from existing text and apply the same formatting to any other text in your presentation, the Format Painter helps you maintain consistency from slide to slide. In addition, it is a real time saver.

Using the Format Painter

1. Select "$2,000,000" on Slide 7.

2. Double-click on the Format Painter 🖌 on the Standard toolbar.

3. Put your mouse pointer over any area of your slide. You mouse should have changed shape. It now looks like an I-Beam carrying a paint brush,

If you can't find the Format Painter, make certain that the Standard toolbar is displayed. Choose View>Toolbars>Standard to put a check mark next to this toolbar.

By double-clicking on the Format Painter you can use it as many times as you want throughout the entire presentation. If you single-click on the Format Painter, you will only be able to use it one time.

4. Select the text "500" in the first line of Slide 7. The formatting from "$2,000,000" is applied to the selected text.

5. Select the remaining numbers in Slide 7 to format the slide as shown.

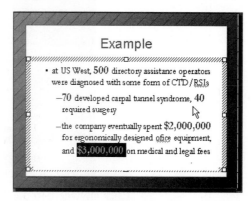

6. Click once on the Format Painter on the Formatting toolbar to turn the Format Painter off.

7. Save your presentation.

Aligning Text

Many of the AutoLayouts available in PowerPoint include placeholders for text. These placeholders are called text boxes and the borders of these boxes serve as margins for the text that you enter in that placeholder. In addition to including a text box, the text alignment has also been established. In other words, when you type text into a specific placeholder, the text will either be aligned at the left, center, or right side of the text box.

There are several ways that you can change the alignment of the text in the text box. One way to change the alignment is to use the alignment buttons on the Formatting toolbar. Another option is to choose Format>Alignment from the Menu bar. There are also keyboard shortcuts for each of the alignment options.

As a general guideline, larger bodies of text such as paragraphs are easier to read when they are left aligned, while titles and headings are usually easier to see when they are centered.

Changing the Text Alignment for All Slides

1. Switch to Slide view.

2. Choose View>Master>Slide Master from the Menu bar.

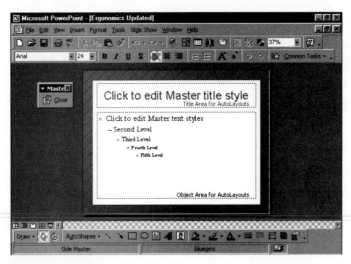

3. Click anywhere in the line of text that reads, "Click to edit Master title style."

4. Choose Format>Alignment>Align Left.

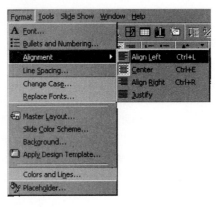

5. Choose View>Normal.

6. Scroll through the slides in your presentation. All of the titles for each slide should appear aligned at the left instead of centered.

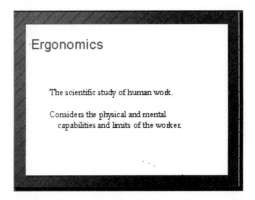

To quickly change the alignment of a paragraph, put your insertion point somewhere in the paragraph that you want to change and choose one of the following shortcuts.

Left Alignment: Control-L, Right Alignment: Control-R, Center Alignment: Control: E.

In reviewing the change you've just made, the original center-aligned titles look better in almost every case. Though you could go back to the Slide Master and change the alignment for the Title placeholder back to Left, a quicker method would be to use Undo.

Undo and Redo

Undo reverses or undoes the last executed command. In addition, PowerPoint 2000 offers multiple-level undo, which means you can reverse the result of multiple commands simply by choosing Undo several times. Each time you choose Undo you will reverse the last command. Commands can only be undone in the order in which they were initially executed.

The number of times you can click the Undo button to reverse a command can be changed. To increase or decrease the number of undos, choose Tools>Options>Edit and use the spin box or up and down arrows in the Maximum number of undos box to change the number.

The keyboard shortcuts for Undo and Redo are Control-Z and Control-Y respectively.

Redo works in reverse. In other words, it undoes the most recent Undo command. Redo is only available if you have used Undo. If you have not used Undo, Redo will be dimmed or grayed out.

Undo and Redo are accessible from Edit on the Menu bar. In addition, because these commands are used so often, Undo and Redo buttons are available on the Standard toolbar. The keyboard shortcut for Undo is Control-Z.

Using Undo to Change the Text Alignment

1. Choose Edit>Undo Align Left.

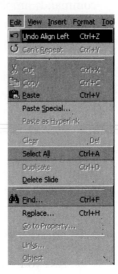

The Slide Master reappears on your screen.

2. Choose View>Normal.

   The slide titles on all of the slides should once again be centered.

3. Go to Slide 1.

4. From the Common Tasks drop-down list box choose Slide Layout and select the Bulleted List AutoLayout (second option in the first row).

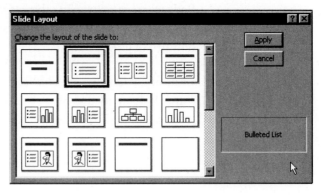

You can also choose Format>Slide Layout from the Menu bar.

5. Choose Apply. The two paragraphs in the lower text box now appear with bullets.

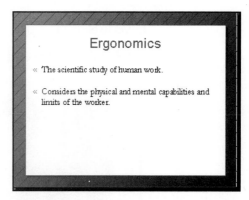

6. Click the Undo button 🔄 on the Standard toolbar. The Bulleted List AutoLayout is removed and the bullets disappear.

7. Click the Redo button 🔄 on the Standard toolbar and the Bulleted List AutoLayout reappears.

8. Save your presentation.

Promoting and Demoting Text

Bulleted lists may contain text at more than one level. This establishes a hierarchy where each level is in a position based on its importance. This structure is called a multilevel bulleted list. This list is basically an outline where one bulleted item appears below and indented to the right of another bulleted item to indicate that it is a subtopic or subordinate to the item above it. In PowerPoint you can have up to five different paragraph levels. However, these lower levels often become hard to read and therefore they may actually distract the audience.

The appearance of the text and the bullet at each level is determined by the slide layout and the design template. You can shift the position or importance of any paragraph or item in the list by promoting or demoting it. Promoting is the process of raising an item from a lower level to a higher level or moving it from right to left. Demoting is the process of lowering an item from a higher level to a lower level which involves moving the item further to the right.

Both the Promote and Demote buttons are available on the Formatting toolbar. The Promote button appears as a left-pointing arrow and the Demote button appears as a right-pointing arrow.

Promoting Text

1. Go to Slide 14.

2. Select the four bulleted items under "Solutions."

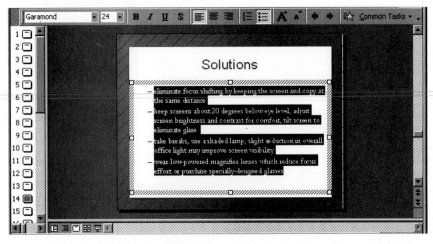

3. Click the Promote button 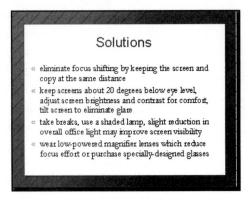 on the Formatting toolbar. All four bulleted items should now appear as shown.

4. Go to Slide 7.

5. Click on the drop-down list box under Common Tasks and choose Slide Layout.

6. From the Slide Layout dialog box, choose Bulleted List (second option, first row) and choose Reapply.

Tab and Shift-Tab can be used to Promote and Demote a bulleted item on a slide.

7. Click anywhere on the first bulleted item that begins, "at US West" and click the Promote button  on the Formatting toolbar.

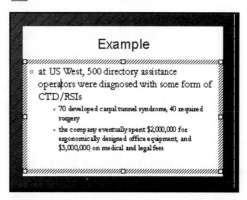

8. Select the remaining two bulleted items in the slide and click the Promote button twice. Pressing the Promote button twice promotes the items two levels so that all three bullets are now aligned and at the same level in the hierarchy. The last two bulleted items should actually appear below or as subtopics to the first bulleted paragraph.

9. With the last two bulleted items still selected, click the Demote button on the Formatting toolbar or press the Tab key. Your slide should appear as shown.

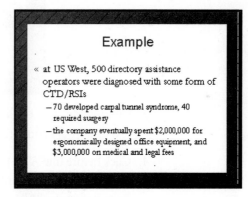

10. Save your presentation.

Cut, Copy, and Paste

Whenever you want to move or copy text either within the same slide or between slides you use cut, copy, and paste. To move text, use cut and paste. To copy text you use copy and paste.

In essence, the process of moving or copying text is almost identical. There are four steps involved any time you cut and paste or copy and paste text. The first step is to select the text that you wish to cut or copy. The next step is to choose Cut or Copy. The third step is to position the insertion point where you want the text to reappear. The final step is to choose Paste.

The keyboard shortcuts for Cut, Copy, and Paste are as follows:

Cut: Control-X

Copy: Control-C

Paste: Control-V

You can also try selecting the text and clicking the right mouse button. You'll see the cut, copy, and paste commands from the context-sensitive menu that appears.

Because cut, copy, and paste are common procedures, Microsoft has given you many ways to execute these commands. Cut, Copy, and Paste can be found under Edit on the Menu bar. In addition, there are buttons on the Standard toolbar that represent each of these commands. Finally, you can use the right mouse button or keyboard shortcuts to execute these common commands.

Whenever you choose Cut or Copy, the selected text is stored in an area of memory called the Clipboard where it will remain until you cut or copy a different selection.

Moving Text in Slide View

1. Go to Slide 3.

2. Select the text in the second bullet.

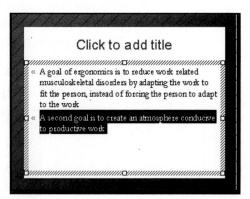

3. Choose Edit>Cut or click on the Cut button ✂ on the Standard toolbar. The text disappears and is temporarily stored on the Clipboard.

4. Click before the "A" in the first bulleted item that reads, "A goal of..." Make certain that the first bulleted item is not selected. There should be an Insertion Point before the "A."

5. Choose Edit>Paste. The paragraph that reads, "A second goal..." should now appear before the paragraph that reads, "A goal of..."

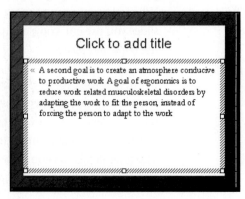

6. Press the Enter key. A second bullet should reappear.

Another way to move text is to use the drag and drop feature. Select the text to be moved. Position the mouse pointer on top of the selected text and drag. A dotted vertical line will appear on the screen. Drag this line to the place where you wish to move the text and release the left mouse button.

7. Change the text so that the slide appears as shown.

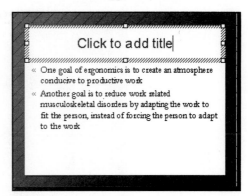

8. Save your presentation.

Moving Text in Outline View

1. Go to Slide 2.

2. Switch to Outline view.

3. Click on the last bulleted item, "Lighting" in Slide 2.

4. If necessary, choose View>Toolbars>Outlining to display the Outlining toolbar in PowerPoint.

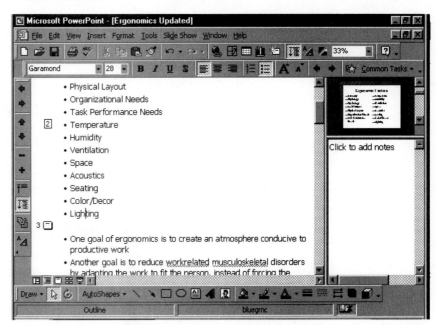

5. Click the Move Up button ↑ on the Outlining toolbar to move "Lighting" above "Color/Decor."

Sometimes it is easier to move slides up and down if the entire presentation doesn't appear in Outline view. You can collapse and expand portions of an outline to view only the text that you need to view at the moment. The Collapse and Expand buttons appear on the Outlining toolbar as a plus and minus respectively.

6. Switch back to Slide view.

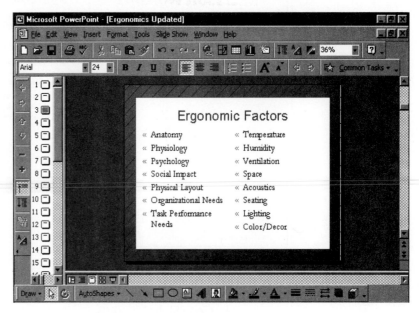

7. Save your presentation.

Copying Text

1. Go to Slide 1.

2. Double click on "Ergonomics" in the Title placeholder to select it.

3. Choose Edit>Copy or click on the Copy button 🖹 on the Standard toolbar.

4. Go to Slide 3.

5. Click anywhere in the Title placeholder that reads, "Click to add title."

6. Choose Edit>Paste or click on the Paste button 🖹 on the Standard toolbar.

7. Click before the "E" in "Ergonomics" and type "Goals of".

Your slide should appear as shown.

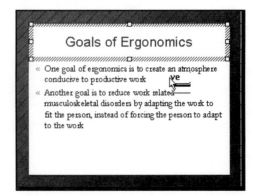

The WordArt toolbar should automatically appear whenever you have a WordArt object selected. If you don't see it, choose View>Toolbars>WordArt to display it.

Microsoft WordArt

Microsoft WordArt is a separate application that comes packaged with PowerPoint. WordArt allows you to create decorative text which can be embedded as an object into your presentation. The special effects that you can apply to text using the WordArt program will add interest and creativity to your slide show.

Fortunately, WordArt is extremely intuitive and simple to use. You can access WordArt from the Drawing toolbar. Once you are in WordArt you simply choose a style and then enter your text.

The WordArt toolbar allows you to modify your WordArt image in a variety of ways. For example, you can rotate it, add shadows or three-dimensional effects, or change its alignment.

Using Microsoft WordArt

1. Go to Slide 1.

2. From the Common Tasks drop-down list box, choose New Slide.

3. From the New Slide dialog box, choose Blank (third row, last option) and click OK.

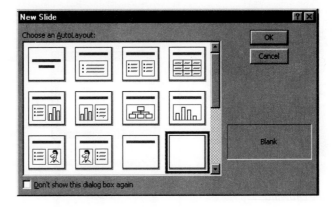

4. Switch to Slide Sorter view.

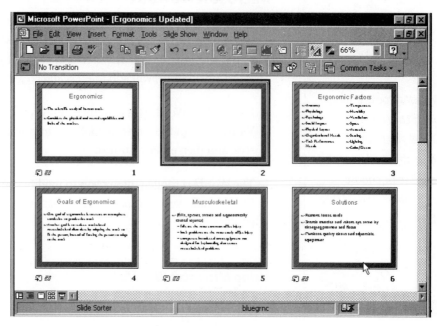

5. Drag Slide 2 (the blank slide) before Slide 1. When you see a long vertical line appear before Slide 1, release the left mouse button. Slide 1 should now be the blank slide.

If you can't find the Drawing toolbar, switch to Slide view and choose View>Toolbars>Drawing.

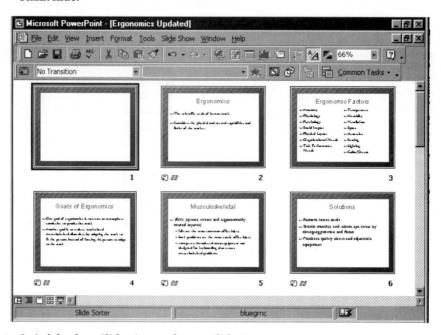

6. Switch back to Slide view and go to Slide 1.

7. Find the Drawing toolbar. It will probably appear at the bottom of your screen.

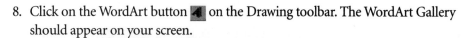

The WordArt toolbar contains a host of buttons that allow you to change the color, position, size, font, style, and shape of a Wordart object. Insert a WordArt object and try these different formatting features to learn more about them.

8. Click on the WordArt button on the Drawing toolbar. The WordArt Gallery should appear on your screen.

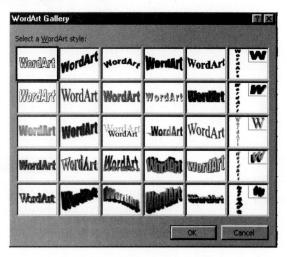

9. From the WordArt Gallery, choose the second option in the third row and click OK.

10. At the Edit WordArt Text dialog box, type "Ergonomics" where it currently says "Your Text Here" and click OK. The WordArt object is now embedded in Slide 1. You should see selection or sizing handles around it.

Manipulating WordArt Objects

1. Position the mouse pointer over the lower right-hand sizing handle until the mouse pointer changes to a double-headed arrow.

2. Drag down and to the right to resize the object.

3. Position the mouse on top of the WordArt object until the mouse pointer changes to a four-headed arrow, which indicates that you can move the object.

4. Drag the object to the center of the slide.

5. Save your presentation.

Text Boxes

Slide AutoLayouts are useful because they already include appropriate placeholders for the text and objects that we often include in a slide. The majority of the time, these AutoLayouts will probably serve your needs. On occasion, however, you may find that you need to add text outside of these existing placeholders.

You can add text outside of an existing text placeholder by inserting a new text box. Just like the text placeholders that are automatically created when you choose an AutoLayout, text boxes can include bulleted lists, titles, notes, and labels.

Inserting a Text Box

1. Go to Slide 1.

2. Click on the Text Box button on the Drawing toolbar.

If you only want to move an object a very slight distance, you can nudge it by using the Arrow keys.

3. Position the mouse in the lower right-hand corner of your slide. Your mouse should look like a crosshair.

4. Drag the crosshair to create a text box approximately the same size as the one shown below.

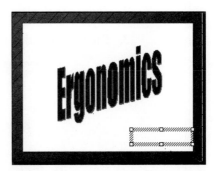

5. An insertion point should appear inside the text box you just created. Type your name in this text box. Don't worry if your name is too long to fit on one line of the box; just keep typing and allow the text to wrap to the next line.

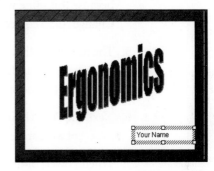

6. Use the sizing handles to resize the box so that all of the text fits on one line.

7. Save your presentation.

Spell Check

As you type text into a placeholder, PowerPoint checks your words against a built-in dictionary. Any word that it can't find in its dictionary is marked with a jagged red underline. You may have noticed jagged red underlines appear underneath some of the words in your slides. These jagged red underlines indicate that the word may be misspelled. These underlines will not appear in Slide Show view or when a presentation is printed. They are merely available as a guide to you — an indication that there may be a problem. This feature of Microsoft PowerPoint is called Spell-It.

In addition to Spell-It, you can also use PowerPoint's built-in dictionary to check the spelling in your presentation after it has been completed. The PowerPoint spell checker works in all views except Slide Show view.

To run the spell checker, choose Tools>Spelling or click on the Spelling button ![spelling button] on the Standard toolbar.

Right-click on any word with a wavy red underline. A context-sensitive menu will appear with suggested spellings as well as the option to run the spelling checker.

Spell Checking the Presentation

1. Switch to Normal View and go to Slide 1.

2. Choose Tools>Spelling.

3. The first word that the PowerPoint dictionary highlights is "workrelated."

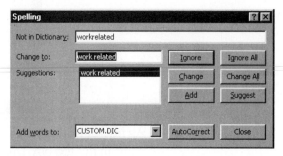

4. The suggestion divides the word into two words. Because this is correct and because this same word may be used throughout the presentation, choose Change All to correct any occurrence of the word "workrelated."

5. The next word that is highlighted is "musculoskeletal." This word is correct. Because this word has been used through the presentation you should choose Ignore All to ignore any occurrence of the word.

6. Next, the PowerPoint dictionary highlights the word "cuases." Choose Change to accept the correct suggestion.

7. When PowerPoint highlights "CTDs" and "RSIs" choose Ignore All.

8. Change "ofice" to "office."

9. When PowerPoint highlights "degress," be certain to click on the correct suggestion, "degrees," before you choose Change.

10. Upon completion, PowerPoint should indicate that the spelling check is complete.

11. Click OK.

12. Save your presentation.

13. Close PowerPoint.

Complete Project C: Mastering Golf

The keyboard shortcut for the spell checker is F7.

CHAPTER 5

WORKING WITH OBJECTS

CHAPTER OBJECTIVE:

To learn how to add interest, variety, and excitement to your presentation by working with and manipulating the different types of objects available in PowerPoint. In Chapter 5 you will:

- Learn how to insert clip art from the ClipArt Gallery.
- Learn to promote and demote in Outline view.
- Understand how to insert photographs and images from various sources.
- Learn how to resize, scale, move, rotate, and crop objects.
- Understand how to create and edit objects with the collection of tools available on the Drawing toolbar.
- Understand how to insert text boxes inside objects.
- Understand how to fill and format objects.
- Learn to group and ungroup objects.

PROJECTS TO BE COMPLETED:

- The Backcountry Almanac
- Fitness Facts
- Mastering Golf
- **Easy & Elegant Baking**
- Wildflower Spas
- Washington Apples Online
- Yard Debris Recycling Program

Working with Objects

An excellent way to add interest, variety, and excitement to your presentation is to incorporate objects into your slides. Objects offer a creative way of visually communicating with your audience as you attempt to entertain, inform, or persuade them. A single graphic such as a photograph or chart can often illustrate what might take pages of text to address. As an added bonus, you can also use images to add humor to your presentation. There are many different ways of incorporating interesting and appropriate graphics into your presentation. In this chapter, you'll learn about several of these methods.

Microsoft ClipArt Gallery

The Microsoft ClipArt Gallery is a collection of hundreds of images that you can use in your PowerPoint presentations without having to obtain permission from the original artist. The ClipArt Gallery is packaged with PowerPoint and many of the images within this gallery are installed when you install PowerPoint. The remaining clip art images are accessible from the original CD.

Inserting ClipArt into a New Slide

1. Start the PowerPoint application.

2. At the initial PowerPoint screen, choose "Blank presentation" and click OK.

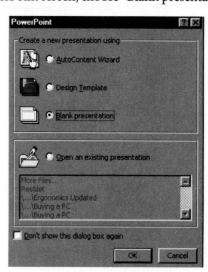

3. At the New Slide dialog box, choose the Title Slide AutoLayout (first option, first row).

4. As shown below, type "Treasures of Wildlife" in the title placeholder and "Your Name" in the subtitle placeholder.

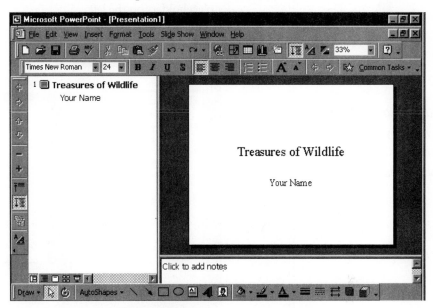

You can also insert a new slide by choosing Insert> New Slide from the Menu bar or using the keyboard shortcut Control-M.

5. Click the New Slide button 🖺 on the Standard toolbar.

By choosing an AutoLayout specifically designed for clip art, PowerPoint makes it easy for you to add images to any slide.

6. From the New Slide dialog box, choose the Text & ClipArt AutoLayout (first option, third row) and click OK.

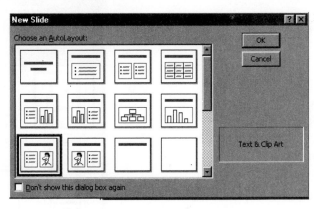

If you don't see the New Slide button, choose View>Toolbars and make certain that there is a check mark next to Standard.

You can also add clip art to any slide layout by choosing Insert>Picture>Clip Art from the Menu bar.

7. Click to add the title, "Gallery of Riches" and the two bulleted items, "Marvelous heritage of wildlife" and "Astounding natural resources" to the bulleted list placeholders on the left.

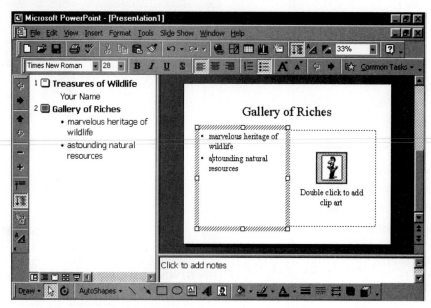

8. Double-click in the placeholder that reads, "Double click to add clip art."

9. From the Microsoft Clip Gallery, click on the Animals category.

You can add any picture to the Clip Gallery. To do so, choose Import Clips on the Clip Gallery toolbar. Select the file you want to add and choose Open. Select a category and choose OK.

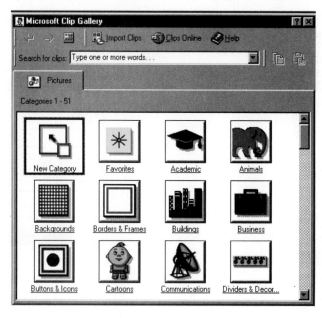

10. From the Animals category, click on the lion (first option, first row).

If you know the name of the clip art image you are hoping to find, a quick way to locate it is to type the name in the Search for clips: text box.

11. From the list of four callouts that appear when you click on the lion, choose Insert clip (the first callout).

The lion now appears in the placeholder on the right side of your slide.

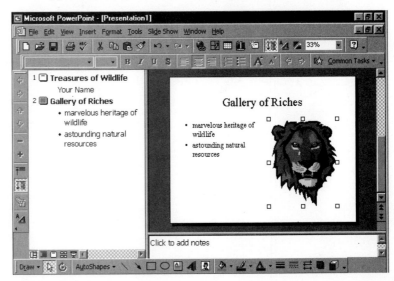

Additional clip art images are available from the Web. Choose Clips Online for access to these images.

12. Choose File>Save As from the Menu bar.

13. Under the Save in drop-down list, navigate to your **Work in Progress** folder.

14. Name the file "Treasures of Wildlife".

15. Click Save and leave this presentation open for the next exercises.

Promoting and Demoting in Outline View

1. With the **Treasures of Wildlife** file open, go to Slide 2.

2. In the Outline to the left side of the slide, click at the end of the second bullet after the word "resources" and press Enter to add a third bullet to Slide 2 of your presentation.

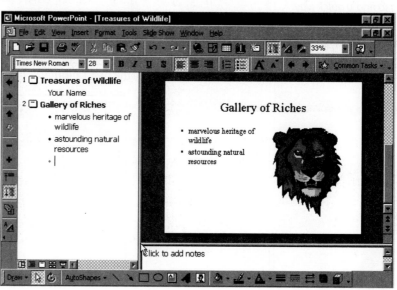

If you do not see the Outline to the left of the slide, choose View>Normal.

If you do not see the Outlining toolbar, choose View>Toolbars>Outlining.

You can also promote in an outline by pressing Shift-Tab. To demote, press the Tab key.

3. From the Outlining toolbar at the left of the outline, click the Promote button to promote the third bullet to a new slide, Slide 5.

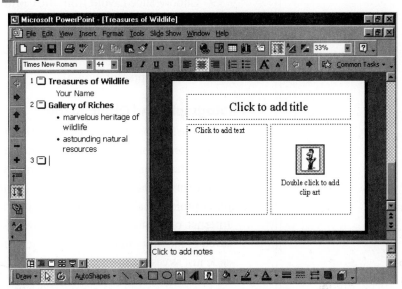

You'll notice that the slide layout from Slide 2 is automatically used for Slide 3 when you add a slide using the Outline.

4. Type "Joys of Wildlife" and press Enter.

PowerPoint automatically inserts a new paragraph at the same level as the previous paragraph. In this case, PowerPoint inserts Slide 4.

5. From the Outlining toolbar at the left of the outline, click the Demote button to demote the fourth slide to a bullet under Slide 3.

6. Type "Cannot be assessed in dollars and cents" and press Enter to add a second bullet.

7. Type "Inherited precious gifts".

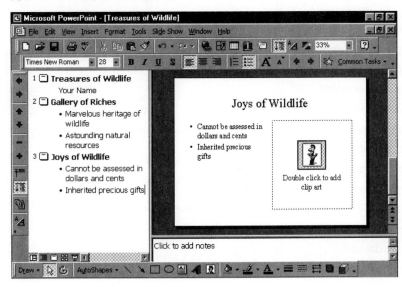

8. Click on the Slide view button on the Views toolbar.

9. Choose Slide Layout from the Common Tasks drop-down menu on the Formatting toolbar.

10. Choose the Bulleted List AutoLayout (second option, first row) and click Apply.

11. Save your presentation.

Photographs and Other Images

Using the Microsoft ClipArt Gallery provides you with a quick way to add graphics to your presentation without creating the images yourself. Though the Microsoft Clip Gallery makes hundreds of clip art images available, there are times when you will want to insert graphics that you have created yourself or purchased as part of some other professional clip art collection, cartoons that you have downloaded from the Internet, or photographs that you have taken with a digital camera or scanned and saved to file. You can insert all of these different types of images into a PowerPoint slide just as easily as you inserted clip art from the Microsoft Clip Gallery.

Inserting Photographs and Images from File

1. Choose Insert>New Slide from the Menu bar.

2. From the New Slide dialog box, choose the Title Only AutoLayout (third option, third row). Click OK.

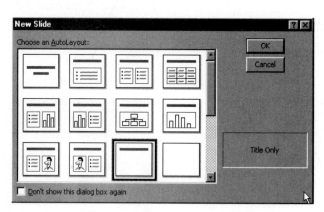

3. Click the title placeholder to add the title "Majestic Elk".

4. Click anywhere within the slide but outside of the title to deselect the title and remove the sizing handles from the title placeholder.

5. Choose Insert>Picture>From File.

All images including photographs and drawings are copyright protected. Do not use another artist's original work in your PowerPoint presentation without first obtaining permission or carefully reading the licensing agreement to ensure that the image is in fact within the public domain.

6. From the Insert Picture dialog box, click on the drop-down list box next to Look in and navigate to the **SF-PowerPoint** folder.

7. Click on **Elk.JPG** and choose Insert.

8. Follow steps 1-7 above to create the three slides shown below.

9. Save your presentation.

When trying to select an appropriate image for your presentation, consider your audience, your purpose, the content of the slide, and the file size of the image.

If you do not see the extension ".JPG" after the elk file, the extensions are not set to show on your computer. That's O.K. Continue with the instructions as they are written.

Apply a Design Template

1. Click on the Common Tasks drop-down menu from the Formatting toolbar.

2. Choose Apply Design Template.

3. Choose Nature from the list of presentation design templates and click Apply.

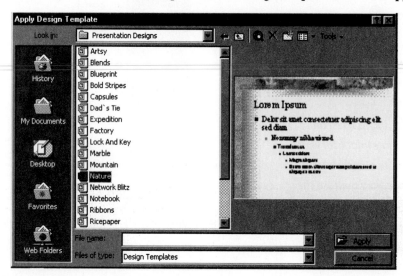

The Picture toolbar contains buttons that allow you to format your images using a variety of different options. For example, you can increase or decrease the brightness and contrast. You can crop, add borders, and recolor the image as well as modify its size and position. Try some of these different options to see how they change your image.

4. Scroll through your slides to see the impact on the placeholders in each slide as a result of applying the Nature design template. Don't worry if some of your photographs or images overlap the text placeholders; we'll fix that later.

5. Save your presentation.

Modifying Objects

PowerPoint provides you with different ways to modify objects. For example, you can resize and scale objects, move objects, change their color, group them with other objects, or apply borders around them. This is merely a fraction from a long list of possibilities. The ability to modify objects allows you to create professional presentations. In the next few steps you'll improve the appearance of your presentation by modifying the objects in your slides using a variety of different techniques.

Moving Objects

1. Go to Slide 4, "Majestic Elk." Notice how the photograph of the elk slightly overlaps the title.

2. Click on the photograph of the elk. You should see selection or sizing handles (small white boxes) appear around the border of the picture.

You can nudge a selected object by using the arrow keys.

3. Position the mouse pointer on top of the photograph. When the mouse changes to a four-headed arrow, drag the photograph down so that it is no longer overlapping the title.

4. With the photograph still selected, choose Format>Picture from the Menu bar.

5. From the Format Picture dialog box, choose the Colors and Lines tab.

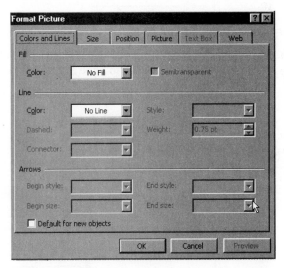

6. Choose Automatic from the Color drop-down list box under Line.

In addition to changing the color of lines and fills, you can also apply patterns. Patterns are particularly useful if you wish to distinguish something in print and you don't have access to a color printer. Using a pattern helps make the distinction obvious.

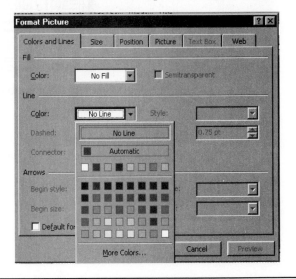

7. Change the Weight to 4 pt. and click OK. A border should appear around the photograph.

8. Follow steps 2-7 to modify and add a border to the photographs in Slides 5-7.

9. Save your presentation.

Resizing ClipArt

1. Go to Slide 2, and if necessary, switch to Slide view.

2. Click on the drop-down list box under Common Tasks and choose Slide Layout.

3. Choose the ClipArt & Text AutoLayout (second option, third row) to switch the clip art to the left side of the slide.

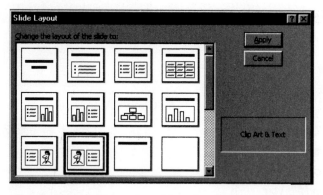

4. Click to select the lion object and position the mouse pointer on the lower-right selection handle.

5. When the mouse pointer changes to a double-headed arrow, drag up and to the left to make the lion's head smaller. It should be approximately half the size of the original.

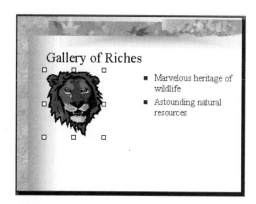

6. Choose Edit>Undo Resize Object to set the size back to the original. You can more accurately resize the object from the Format Picture dialog box.

7. With the lion still selected, choose Format>Picture from the Menu bar.

8. Click on the Size tab.

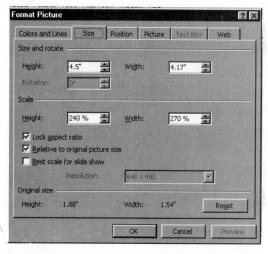

9. Make certain that there is a check mark in the Lock aspect ratio checkbox. This will keep the lion in proportion by automatically adjusting the width if you change the height and vice versa.

10. Change the Height to 2.5″ and click OK.

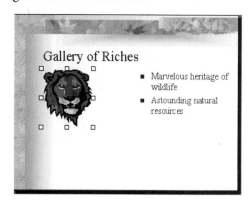

11. Save your presentation.

To maintain the original proportions of the image, hold down the Shift key as you drag a selection handle to resize an image.

Resizing and Moving Text Boxes

1. Click anywhere on the bulleted items at the right of the slide to select the text box or placeholder. Selection or sizing handles should appear around the placeholder just as they appeared around the lion.

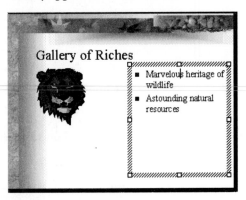

2. Drag the middle left selection handle to the left to make the text box wider.

3. Drag the lower middle selection handle up to make the text box shorter.

4. Position the mouse pointer on top of the text box until the mouse changes to a four-headed arrow and then move the text box down as shown.

The aspect ratio is used to maintain the object's original proportions. In addition to using the Shift key with a sizing handle to maintain an object's original proportion, the addition of the Control key will provide a sizing handle that will proportionally scale an object from the center out. Adding the "A" key will allow you to scale an object vertically, horizontally, or diagonally from the center out. Try each one to get a better idea of how these options work.

5. Save your presentation.

Cropping a Picture

One way to clean up an image or photograph is to remove portions of the image that don't add to it. For example, if you want the focus of a photograph to be on a person or animal, you might want to remove some of the unnecessary background. This is called cropping.

1. Go to Slide 7.

2. Click on the photograph of the pelican to select it.

3. If the Picture toolbar doesn't appear on your screen, choose View>Toolbars>Picture.

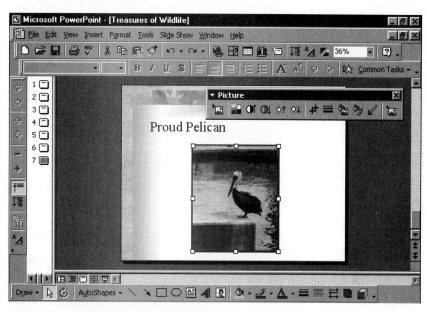

4. Click on the Crop tool [crop] on the Picture toolbar.

5. Position your mouse on the top middle selection handle. The mouse should change shape and should now look like the Crop tool you just selected.

6. Drag the Crop tool down to the water line to remove or "crop" the dock out of the photograph.

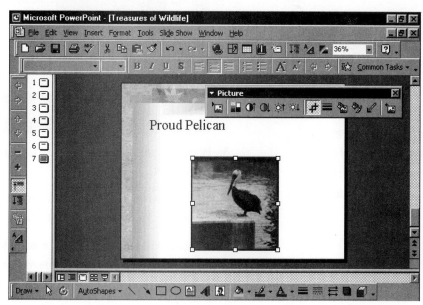

7. Click on the Crop tool on the Picture toolbar to turn it off or deselect it.

8. Move the photograph of the pelican back to the center of the slide.

9. Save your presentation.

As you are making these changes, don't forget the Undo button. It's a handy way to correct a mistake.

Drawing Tools

On the Drawing toolbar, you will find a collection of tools that can be used to create and edit objects from lines, circles, boxes, and AutoShapes. Although PowerPoint is not a drawing program, the Drawing toolbar provides you with the basic tools or building blocks needed to enhance or create simple drawings.

In addition, the Draw menu gives you access to an even larger set of commands for manipulating objects. From this menu you'll find commands that allow you to group or ungroup objects, rotate or flip objects, and align objects.

Creating Images Using the Drawing Toolbar

1. With the Treasures of Wildlife presentation still open, Go to Slide 3.

2. From the Drawing toolbar, click on AutoShapes.

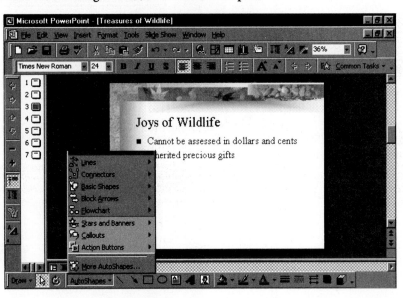

If the Picture toolbar is covering a portion of the slide, you can move it by dragging the blue title bar.

3. Point to Basic Shapes from the menu and click on the Cube (second option, fourth row).

4. Position the mouse pointer, which now appears as a crosshair, in the center of the slide below the last line of text.

5. Drag down to draw a cube approximately the same size as the one shown in the following image. If necessary, move the image to position it as shown.

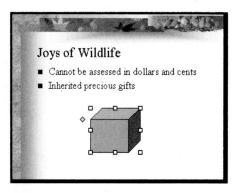

If the Drawing toolbar isn't showing at the bottom of your slide, choose View>Toolbars>Drawing to display it.

6. Click on AutoShapes and choose Basic Shapes.

7. Choose the Heart (first option, sixth row).

8. Drag the crosshair to draw a small heart at the side of the cube.

9. Repeat steps 6-8 to draw several hearts around the cube and throughout the slide. Feel free to get creative by varying the size and position of the hearts.

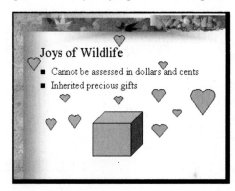

10. Save your presentation and keep it open for the next exercises.

Inserting Text Boxes Inside Objects

1. Click on the Text Box tool 📧 on the Drawing toolbar.

2. Position the crosshair at the left side of the cube and drag to the right to draw a text box as shown.

3. Type "Gift" in the text box.

4. Click on the Center Align button  on the Formatting toolbar to center the word "Gift" inside the text box.

5. Click anywhere outside of the text box to deselect it.

6. Save your presentation.

Filling and Formatting Objects

1. Click on one of the hearts to select it.

2. Click on the drop-down arrow next to the Fill Color button  on the Drawing toolbar.

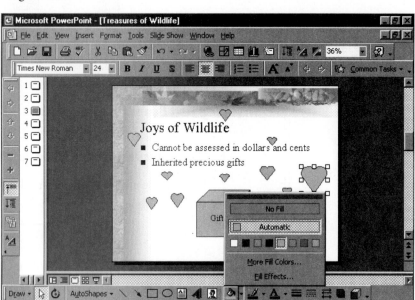

If at any time you need to delete an object, simply click on it, and when selection handles appear around it, press the Delete key.

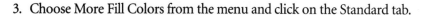

To center align the text you can also choose Format>Alignment>Center or Control-E.

3. Choose More Fill Colors from the menu and click on the Standard tab.

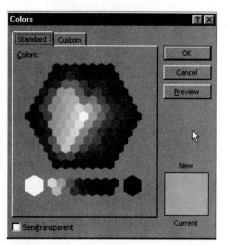

4. Click on any color in the grid and click OK to fill the heart with the color you've selected.

5. Repeat steps 1-4. Fill the hearts with as many different colors as you'd like.

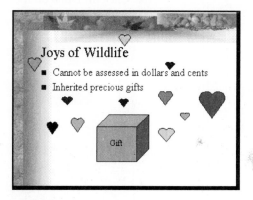

6. Save your presentation.

Grouping and Ungrouping Objects

Every object you create is independent of the other objects on the slide. There are times when you may wish to work with the separate objects as if they were one. For example, if you want to move all of the objects but keep them in the same position to each other, it would be easier to group the objects first and then move them as if they were one object. In addition, if you are creating your own images by piecing together several different objects, you can do this by grouping the objects together as one.

Once you group the objects, if you wish to work with them independently again, you can simply ungroup them. Many clip art images are actually independent objects that have been grouped together. It's possible that a clip art image of a person may be the sum parts of a head, torso, arms, and legs. By ungrouping the object, you can use the arms or legs independent of the torso and head.

From the Fill Effects option you'll see that you can fill an object with textures, gradients, patterns, and even pictures.

Grouping Objects

1. Go to Slide 3.

2. Hold down the Shift key and click on the cube and the text box to select both of these drawing objects.

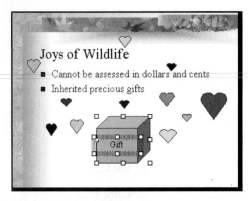

3. Click on Draw on the Drawing toolbar.

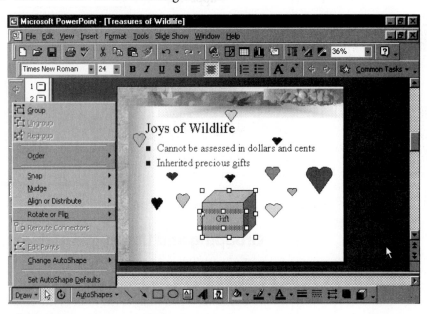

4. Choose Group from the Draw menu.

   The selection handles will disappear from the text box because the text box and the cube are now considered one object.

5. Position the mouse pointer on top of the cube. When the mouse changes to a four-headed arrow, drag the cube to slightly move it down on the slide.

If Group is dimmed or grayed out, hold down the Shift key and click on all of the objects that you want to group together.

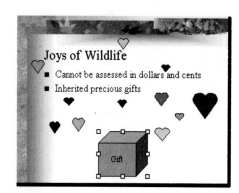

6. Save your presentation.

Rotating Objects

1. Go to Slide 3. Click on the cube to select it.

2. Choose the Free Rotate button 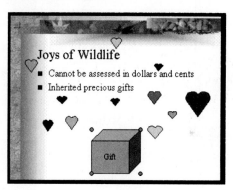 on the Drawing toolbar. Green circles should appear at the corners of the cube.

3. Position the mouse on top of the upper-right circle. The mouse will change shape and will look like the Free Rotate button you just selected.

4. Drag down to rotate the cube.

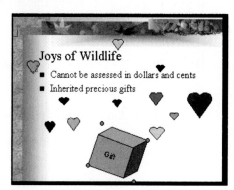

5. Click on the Free Rotate button to turn it off.

6. Save your presentation.

In addition to using the Free Rotate button, there are other rotation options available from the Draw menu on the Drawing toolbar. Choose Draw>Rotate or Flip to examine some of these options.

You can view your slide show in Slide Show view at any time by using the keyboard shortcut F5.

Ungrouping Objects

Now that you have moved and rotated the object as one item, you can ungroup it again.

1. If necessary, click on the cube to select it.

2. Choose Ungroup from the Draw menu.

    Once again you should see selection handles around both the cube and the text box indicating that these are independent objects.

3. Click anywhere outside of the cube to deselect it.

4. Click on the "Gift" text box to select it.

5. Click on the Free Rotate button on the Drawing toolbar and rotate the text box so that it is parallel to the cube.

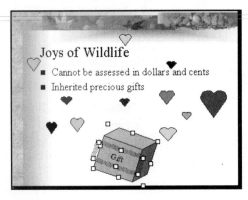

6. Click on the Free Rotate button again to turn it off or deselect it.

7. Go to Slide 1 and choose Slide Show view to view your presentation.

8. Save, Close, and Exit your presentation and PowerPoint.

Complete Project D: Easy & Elegant Baking

REVIEW #1

CHAPTERS 1 THROUGH 5:

In Chapters 1 through 5, you learned to follow a sequence of stages that will help you prepare, organize, and deliver an effective presentation. You became familiar with PowerPoint's tools. You learned how to modify an existing presentation. You studied the different methods for adding text to your presentation. And finally, you learned how to work with objects to enhance your presentation. Through this series of discussions, extensive hands-on activities, and projects, you should:

- Know how to define your purpose by learning what type of information will be most useful to your audience. You should understand that you need to develop your topic by realizing that your purpose and topic are intertwined, and that you must research your subject to develop an effective presentation. You should also understand that you must analyze your audience so that you can tailor your presentation to meet its wants and needs.

- Know how to launch PowerPoint, and have a solid understanding of the PowerPoint Working Environment. You should understand how to create a blank presentation and how to add slides to your presentation with AutoLayout. You should know how to save, open, and close a presentation.

- Have developed a solid understanding of how to add text to an existing presentation that needs updating. You should know how to find and replace text in your presentation. You should have learned how to reorder slides in Slide Sorter View, as well as having learned how to navigate among different views.

- Be familiar with entering text in different views. You should understand line spacing of your text; how to change fonts on all slides, as well as individual slides; how and when to use Undo and Redo; understand how to create text boxes; and know how to check spelling. You should have become familiar with the methods of changing the alignment of text in a text box either by using the alignment buttons on the Formatting toolbar, by choosing Format>Align from the Menu bar, or by using keyboard shortcuts.

- Know how to insert clip art from the ClipArt Gallery, as well as know how to insert photographs and images from other sources. You should know how to resize, scale, move, rotate, and crop objects. You should be familiar with the Drawing toolbar, while understanding how to use it to create and edit objects.

ENHANCING YOUR PRESENTATION

CHAPTER OBJECTIVE:

To learn some of the additional features that allow you to enhance your PowerPoint presentations. You will learn that at times you will need to combine several presentations into one. In Chapter 6 you will:

- Learn to create a new presentation from existing slides.
- Learn how to import text created in other applications such as Microsoft Word.
- Learn that the most effective way to organize lists and columns of information.
- Understand how to modify the table structure.
- Become familiar with Add AutoNumber bullets.
- Understand how to customize bullets.
- Learn how to wrap text in a text box.
- Understand how to add slide transitions.
- Learn how to add animation.
- Become familiar with adding speaker's notes.

PROJECTS TO BE COMPLETED:

- The Backcountry Almanac
- Fitness Facts
- Mastering Golf
- Easy & Elegant Baking
- Wildflower Spas
- Washington Apples Online
- Yard Debris Recycling Program

Enhancing Your Presentation

Importing Text

At times you will find the need to combine several presentations into one. You may also want to create a presentation from an existing document such as an outline for a research report that might have been created in a word processing program such as Microsoft Word. Though you could retype the information from one presentation or document into a new presentation, PowerPoint also allows you to import these files or portions of these files directly into a new or existing presentation.

Although it's not possible for PowerPoint to import documents created in any and all applications, it is feasible to assume that PowerPoint may recognize some of the different file formats you are using. Consequently, importing files is certainly worth pursuing, particularly if the presentation is quite lengthy.

Importing Text From a PowerPoint File

1. From the **SF-PowerPoint folder**, open the **VacationClub1** file.

2. Go to Slide 2, the last slide in this presentation.

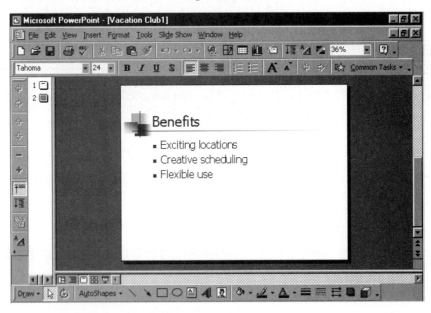

3. Choose Insert>Slides from Files.

4. Click Browse from the Slide Finder dialog box.

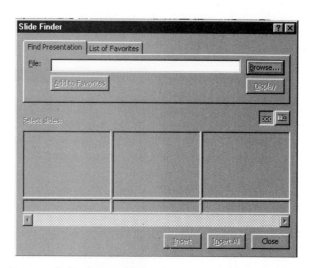

5. From the Browse dialog box Look in: the **SF-PowerPoint** folder.

6. Click on **Vacation Club2** and choose Open.

7. Choose Insert All at the bottom of the Slide Finder dialog box and then choose Close.

The three slides from **Vacation Club2** should be added to the **Vacation Club1** presentation. **Vacation Club1** should now have a total of five slides.

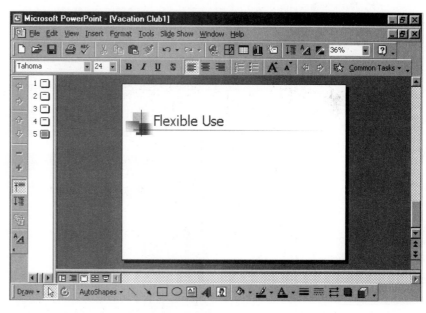

When you insert slides from one presentation into another, the design template applied to the original presentation (the one the slides are being inserted into) is maintained and applied to all of the slides.

8. Choose File>Save As.

In addition to importing text from PowerPoint, Word, or some other application, you can also export a PowerPoint outline by choosing File>Send To.

8. At the Save As dialog box, rename the file "Vacation Club of America" and save it into your **Work in Progress** folder.

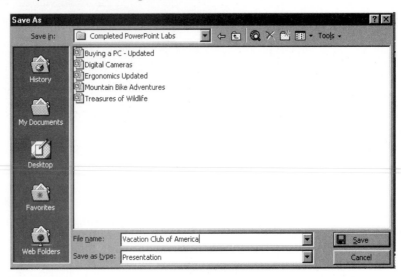

9. Click Save.

10. Leave the presentation open for the following exercises.

Importing Text from Microsoft Word

1. Go to Slide 5.

2. Choose Insert>Slides From Outline.

3. At the Insert Outline dialog box Look in: the **SF-PowerPoint** folder. Click on the **Vacation Club3** file and choose Insert.

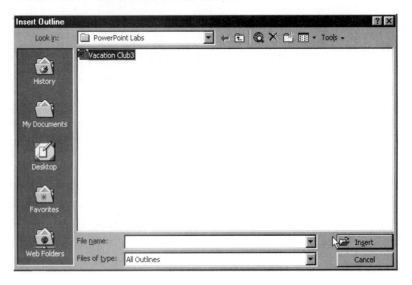

If you just wanted to pull text from Word into the current slide only, you would choose Insert>Object and then Create From File. At the File dialog box, you would choose Browse and then choose the file that contains the text to insert.

To start a new presentation using a Word outline, choose File>Open and change the Files of Type drop-down list box to All Outlines. Click on the appropriate file and choose Open.

The three slides from **Vacation Club3** should be added to the **Vacation Club of America** presentation. **Vacation Club of America** should now have a total of eight slides.

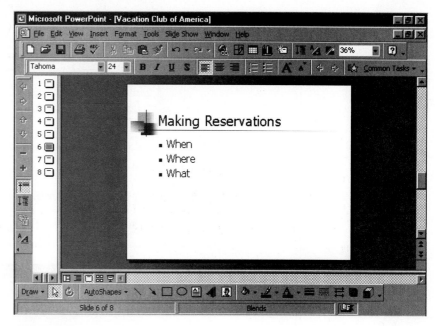

4. Save your presentation.

Creating Tables in PowerPoint

The best way to organize lists and columns of information is to use a table. Tables allow you to organize your content into rows and columns. The intersection between a row and a column is called a cell. Cells can contain text or objects and can have a variety of different sizes and formats. This makes them an extremely flexible method of organizing information that needs to be presented in a concise format.

Microsoft has given you several different ways to insert tables into a slide. You can either choose the Table AutoLayout from the New Slide or Slide Layout dialog boxes or you can choose Table>Insert Table from the Tables and Borders toolbar.

Adding a Table

1. Go to Slide 3 of your presentation.

2. Choose Slide Layout from the Common Tasks drop-down list box on the Formatting toolbar.

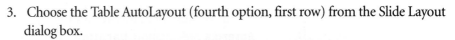

You can also add a table from the Menu bar. Choose Insert>Table.

3. Choose the Table AutoLayout (fourth option, first row) from the Slide Layout dialog box.

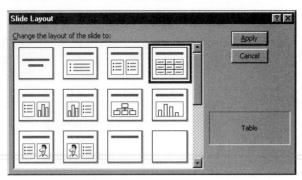

4. Choose Apply.

5. Double-click on the placeholder that reads, "Double click to add table."

6. At the Insert Table dialog box, set the Number of columns: spin box to 2 and the Number of rows: spin box to 6. Click OK.

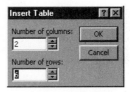

You don't have to use the spin box to enter the number. Sometimes it is faster to simply type the number in the text box and press Enter.

A two-column, six-row table should appear in the placeholder, and the Tables and Borders toolbar should appear on your screen.

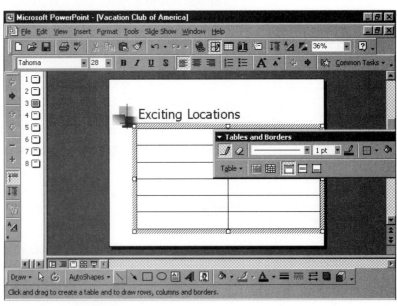

7. Save your presentation.

Adding Text to a Table

1. Click on the "x" in the upper right-hand corner of the Tables and Borders toolbar to close it.

2. In the first cell of the table, type "Resort Name".

3. Press Tab to move to the next cell and type "Resort Location".

4. Press Tab to move to the first cell of the next row and type "Sundance Resort".

5. Press Tab to move to the next cell and type "Whistler, British Columbia". Notice that the text automatically word-wraps to the next line when the column is not wide enough to display all of the text on one line.

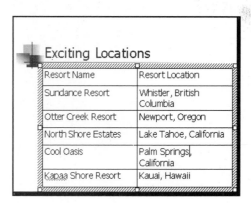

6. Continue adding text to the table as shown.

There are many keyboard shortcuts that can be used to navigate a table.

Tab allows you to move to the next cell. If you are in the last cell of the table, Tab will insert a new row.

Shift-Tab is used to move to the previous cell.

Alt-End takes you to the last cell in the current row. Alt-Home takes you to the first cell in the current row.

7. Save your presentation.

Modifying the Table Structure

Once you've created a table and added text to it, you may need to modify the table structure. For example, you might want to add rows and column or change the height of rows and the width of columns. In addition, you may need to merge or splits cells within a table. With PowerPoint you can accomplish all of these tasks.

Adding and Removing Table Rows

To delete the contents of a cell or cells, simply select the contents and press the Delete or Backspace keys to remove the text. To remove a row or column and not just the text inside the cells, choose Table>Delete Row or Delete Column.

1. Choose View>Toolbars>Tables and Borders.

2. If the Tables and Borders toolbar is covering up the table, move it out of the way by dragging the blue title bar that reads, "Tables and Borders."

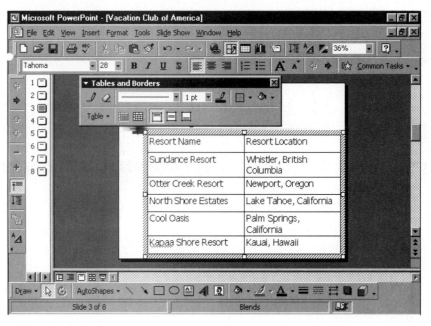

3. Click anywhere in the row that reads, "Cool Oasis."

4. Choose Table>Delete Rows from the Tables and Borders toolbar.

5. Click immediately after "Hawaii" in the last cell of the table.

6. Press Tab to add a new, blank row to the end of the table.

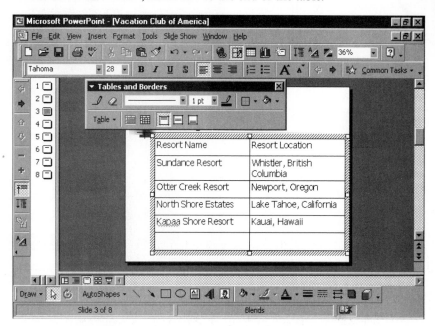

7. Type "Coral Baja Resort", press Tab to move to the next cell, and type "Cabo San Lucas, Mexico".

8. Click anywhere in row two, which reads "Sundance Resort".

9. Choose Table>Insert Rows Above from the Tables and Borders toolbar.

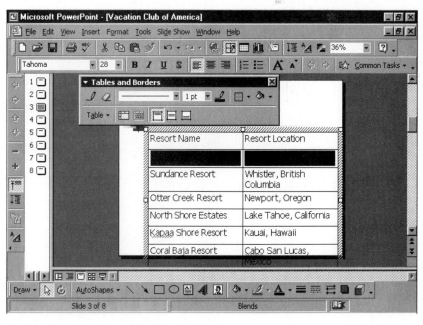

10. Type "Bavarian Retreat", press Tab, and type "Leavenworth, Washington".

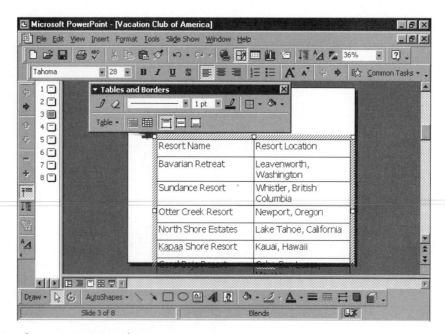

If you made any typing errors, select the text and retype it.

11. Save your presentation.

Changing Column Width and Row Height

1. Position the mouse pointer on the left, middle sizing handle.

2. Drag to the left to resize the table as shown.

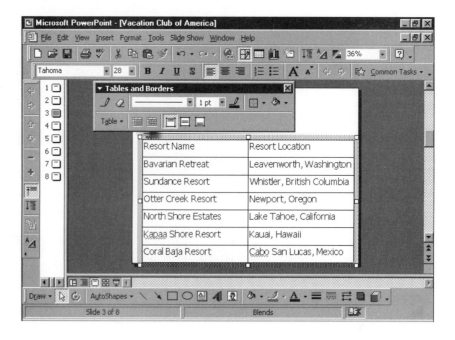

3. Position the mouse pointer on the line that separates Column A and Column B. The mouse should change shape to a double-vertical line with a double-headed arrow. This mouse shape indicates that you now can drag to resize the columns.

4. Drag the mouse to the left to resize the columns. Column B should now be wider than Column A.

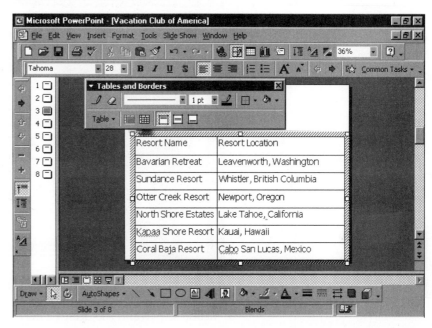

5. Press the Right Arrow key several times to nudge the table to the right of the slide so that the distance between the left edge of the slide and the text in Column A is approximately the same as the distance between the right edge of the slide and Column B.

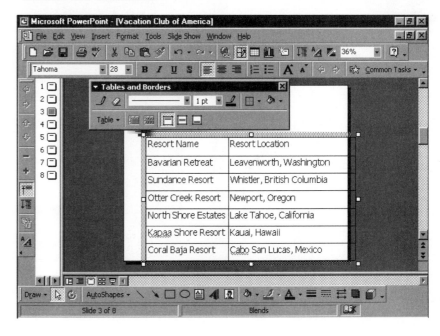

Columns are labeled with letters while rows are labeled with numbers. The first column in a table is Column A. The first row in a table is Row 1.

6. Position the mouse pointer on the horizontal line that separates Row 2 from Row 3. The shape of the mouse will change to a double-horizontal line with a double-headed arrow.

7. Drag the mouse up to decrease the row height as shown.

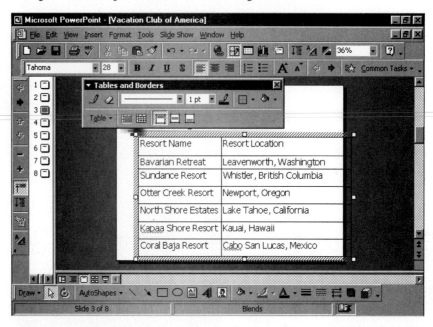

8. Repeat steps 6 and 7 to decrease the row height of rows 3-7. Row 1 should remain unchanged.

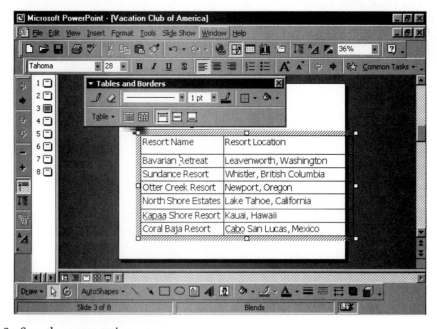

9. Save the presentation.

Revising a Table

Once you have created a table and entered text into it, you can revise the contents and change the appearance as necessary. To modify the contents of a table, select the text to be changed and apply the appropriate formatting.

Aligning Text Within a Table

1. Click anywhere in Row 1 of the table.

2. Choose Table>Select Row from the Tables and Borders toolbar.

3. Click on the Center Vertically button ▤ to vertically center the text within the cells.

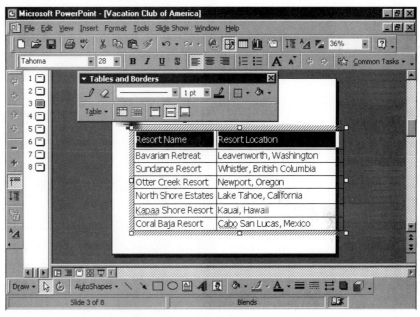

4. Click on the Center button ▤ on the Formatting toolbar to horizontally center the text within the cells.

5. Save your presentation.

Formatting Text

1. With Row 1 still selected, click on the Bold button on the Formatting toolbar.

2. Click on the drop-down list box next to the Font size button and choose 32 pts.

3. Click on the drop-down list box next to the Font Color button **A** ▾ and choose the blue swatch (fourth option).

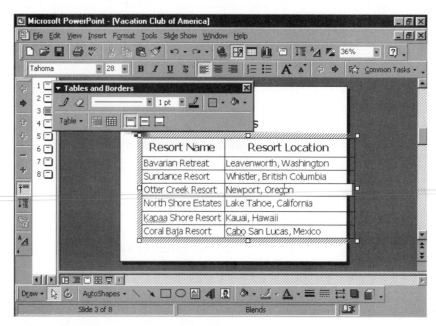

4. Position the mouse pointer on top of the far right table border. When the mouse changes to a double-vertical line with a double-headed arrow, drag it to the left so that the table fits within the slide.

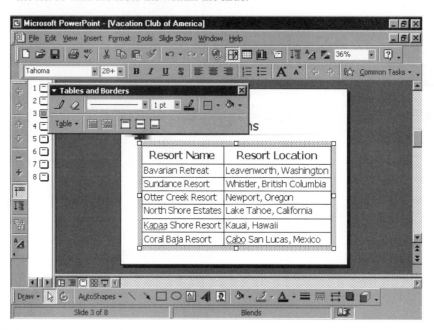

5. Save your presentation.

Adding Borders and Shading to a Table

Borders and shading can be used within and around table cells to add emphasis or visual interest.

1. Click on the drop-down list box next to the Border Width button from the Tables and Borders toolbar and choose 4 1/2 pt.

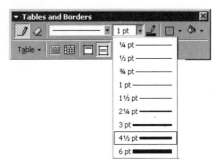

2. The mouse should now be shaped like a pencil and the Draw Table button on the Tables and Borders toolbar should appear depressed.

3. Click at the top left corner of the table and drag to the top right corner of the table to draw a 4 1/2 pt. top border.

4. Repeat Step 3 to draw a 4 1/2 pt. border around all sides of the table.

5. Draw a 4 1/2 pt. border between the first and second row and also between the first and second columns for the first row to separate the header row from the other rows in the table.

6. Click anywhere in Row 1.

7. Choose Table>Select Row from the Tables and Borders toolbar.

8. Choose Table>Borders and Fill from the Tables and Borders toolbar.

9. At the Format Table dialog box, click on the Fill tab.

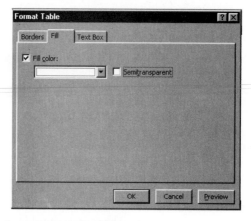

10. Check the Semitransparent checkbox.

11. Click on the drop-down list box under Fill Color: and click on the teal swatch (fifth option). Click OK.

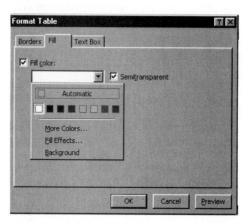

12. Click anywhere outside of the table to deselect Row 1 and view the results of the shading you just applied.

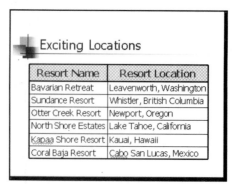

13. Save your presentation.

Bulleted Lists

Speakers will often choose bulleted lists as a way to present information because bulleted lists offer an excellent way to highlight the main points of a presentation. When you choose a slide layout that includes a bulleted list, PowerPoint will automatically use a default bullet style based on the layout and template you've selected. However, at any point, you can turn bullets on and off. In addition, you can change the style of the bullet or even change the bullet to a number.

Changing the Bullet Character

1. Go to Slide 4 of the **Vacation Club of America** presentation.

2. Click on the Common Tasks drop-down list box on the Formatting toolbar and choose Slide Layout.

3. Choose the Bulleted List AutoLayout (second option, first row) from the Slide Layout dialog box and choose Apply.

4. Type the following text as shown below to complete the slide.

The Semitransparent checkbox makes the fill color lighter so that the text is easier to read. This is particularly useful if you have selected a dark color. In order to choose Semitransparent, the Fill color checkbox must be checked.

5. Position the mouse pointer on the top middle sizing handle of the bulleted list placeholder. When the mouse changes to a double-headed arrow, drag down to resize the placeholder.

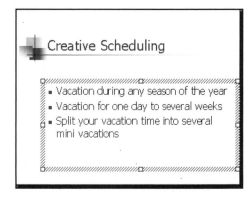

6. Select the three bulleted items that you just typed in Slide 4.

7. Choose Format>Bullets and Numbering from the Menu bar.

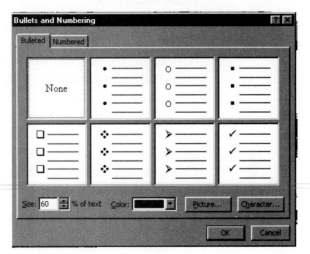

8. Click on the second option, second row.

9. From the drop-down-list box under Color, choose Red.

10. Set the size to 100% of text.

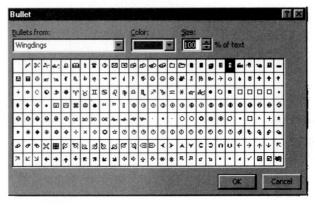

11. Click OK.

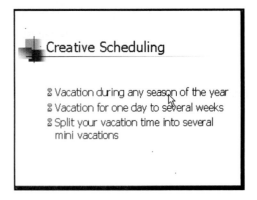

12. Save your presentation and continue with it open.

Adding AutoNumber Bullets

1. Go to Slide 6.

2. Select the three bulleted items in the lower placeholder.

3. Click the Numbering button 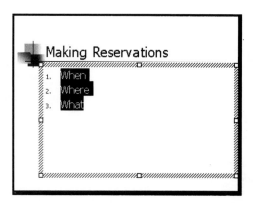 on the Formatting toolbar to change the bullets to numbers.

4. Choose Format>Bullets and Numbering.

5. At the Bullets and Numbering dialog box, click on the Numbered tab and use the spin box to set the Size to 100% of text.

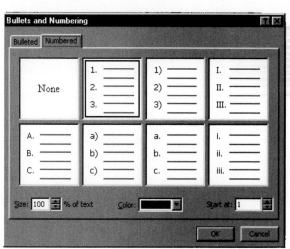

6. Click OK.

7. Save your presentation.

Wrapping Text in a Text Box

1. Go to Slide 5.

2. Choose Insert>Text Box.

3. Position the mouse in the left corner of the slide. When the crosshair appears, drag to create a text box approximately the size of the one shown below.

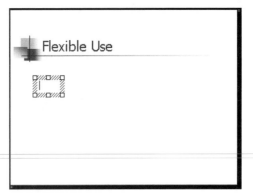

4. Type "Exchange It" and allow the text to wrap to the next line.

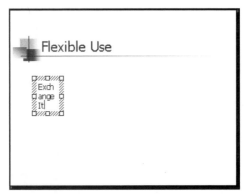

5. Use the middle-right sizing handle to resize the text box so that "Exchange" appears on the first line and "It" appears on the second line.

6. Click on the Center button on the Formatting toolbar to center the text inside the text box.

7. Repeat steps 1-5 to add the text boxes as shown below.

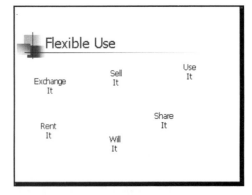

8. Save your presentation.

Don't worry if your text boxes don't appear in the exact same place as the text boxes shown in the slide.

Slide Transitions

When you are giving an on-screen slide show using PowerPoint, you might want to consider adding some of the special effects available in this program. One of these special effects is slide transitions. Slide transitions allows you to apply a special effect that appears as you move from one slide to the next.

Slide transitions will make your presentation appear more professional. In addition, the transitions can be used to grab the attention of the audience as you move from one main topic to the next.

The default slide transition used in PowerPoint is the disappearance of one slide and the appearance of the next. To apply a different slide transition, switch to Slide Sorter view and choose one of the transitions from the Slide Transition Effects drop-down list box on the Slide Sorter toolbar.

Adding Slide Transitions

1. Go to Slide 1 of the **Vacation Club of America** presentation and switch to Slide Show view.

2. Click the left mouse button to move from slide to slide until you have completely viewed the entire presentation.

3. Switch to Slide Sorter view.

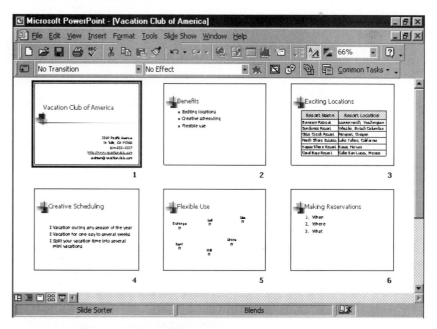

You should notice that a dark border appears around one of the slides, probably Slide 1. This dark border indicates the active or selected slide. If you apply a slide transition, it will only be applied to the selected slide. If you wish to have slide transitions applied to all of the slides in your presentation, be certain to select all of the slides before applying the transition.

4. Choose Edit>Select All to select all of the slides in the presentation. Notice that a dark border now appears around all of the slides.

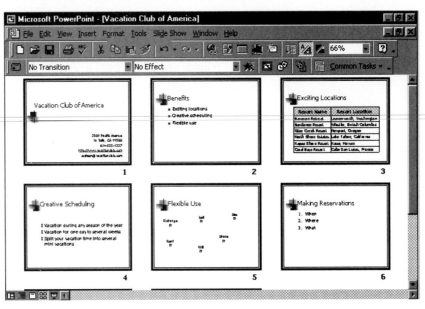

You can also add a slide transition from the Menu bar. Choose Slide Show>Slide Transition.

5. Click on the Slide Transition Effects drop-down list box from the Slide Sorter toolbar.

6. Choose Checkerboard Across.

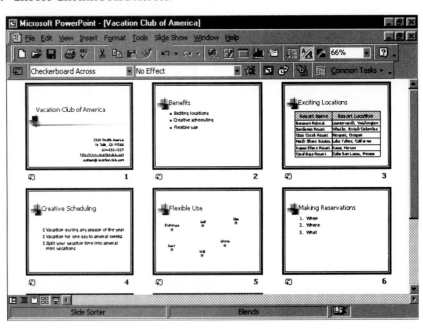

The keyboard shortcut to select all of the slides in a presentation is Control-A.

7. An icon of a slide with an arrow should appear in the lower-left corner of each slide. This icon indicates that a transition has been applied to the slide. Click on any of the icons to see the Checkerboard Across Transition Effect that you just applied.

8. Save your presentation.

9. Switch to Slide Show view and run the slide show in its entirety to get a better idea of how these transitions look.

Animation

Transitions are special effects that are applied from one slide to the next. PowerPoint also allows you to apply special effects to the text and objects within a slide. This is called Animation. The animation you apply determines how and when objects on a slide appear. For example, it's often helpful to have bulleted items appear one at a time. A presenter can fully discuss one bullet or subtopic before moving on to the next. This keeps the audience focused on what the presenter is discussing rather than tempting the audience to read the next bulleted item.

Applying Simple Animation

1. Switch to Slide Sorter view.

2. Choose Edit>Select All.

3. Click on the Preset Animation drop-down list box on the Slide Sorter toolbar.

4. Choose Fly From Left.

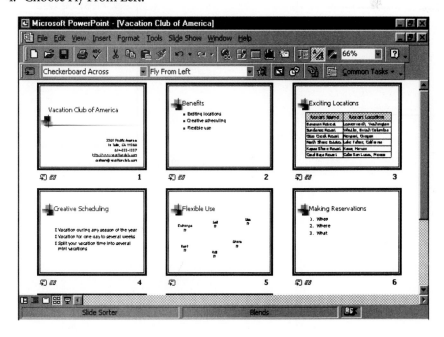

You should now see another icon in the lower-left corner of any slide that includes a bulleted list. This icon indicates that animation has been applied to the objects within the slide. Click on one of the animation icons to view the impact of applying animation to that slide.

5. Save your presentation.

6. Switch to Slide Show view and run your slide show in its entirety to get a better understanding of how the animation impacts your presentation.

Custom Animation

You might have noticed that Slide 5 doesn't include any animation even though you selected all of the slides when you applied the animation. Simple animation effects applied using the Preset Animation drop-down list box will only affect bulleted items within a slide. If you wish to apply animation to other text and objects on a slide, you must do so through the Custom Animation dialog box.

Applying Custom Animation

1. Switch to Slide view.

2. Go to Slide 5.

3. Hold down the Shift key and click on each of the text boxes to select all six of them.

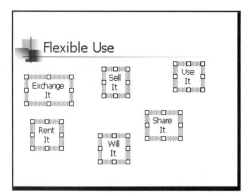

4. Choose Slide Show>Custom Animation.

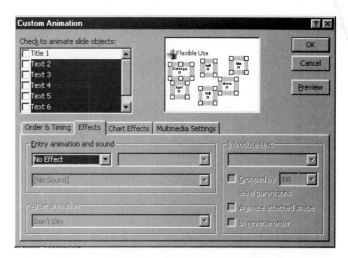

5. Put a check mark in the checkbox next to Title 1 and Text 2-7 under **Check to animate slide objects**.

6. Under Entry animation and sound, choose Appear from the first drop-down list box and Camera from the second drop-down list box.

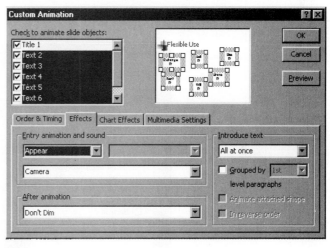

7. Click OK.

8. Switch to Slide Show view and click the mouse to see the impact of the custom animation that you just applied to Slide 5. To view the full impact of the custom animation, continue clicking the left mouse, until the slide show progresses to the next slide.

   If your computer is equipped with a sound card and speakers, in addition to seeing the text boxes appear on the screen one by one, you will also hear the snap of a camera as each text box appears on the slide.

9. Save your presentation and return to Slide 1. View the entire presentation in Slide Show view.

By default, the Preset Animation and Transition is set to "No Effect" and "No Transition".

Speaker's Notes

Although PowerPoint serves as a most useful visual aid and guide to both the speaker and the audience, delivering a professional presentation requires more than just flipping from one slide to the next. The speaker should avoid merely reading the slide to the audience. Instead, the slides should serve as an aid from which the speaker can embellish and add meaning to the points that appear.

A helpful tool for the presenter is Speaker's Notes. Speaker's Notes can be added to the bottom of each slide. The speaker prints a copy of the Speaker's Notes, which include a smaller visual of the slide as well as any added thoughts, comments, and notes that the speaker wishes to share with the audience. The audience doesn't see the notes, but they are an extremely useful part of the presentation nonetheless.

Adding Speaker's Notes

1. Go to Slide 1 of your presentation.

2. Switch to Normal view.

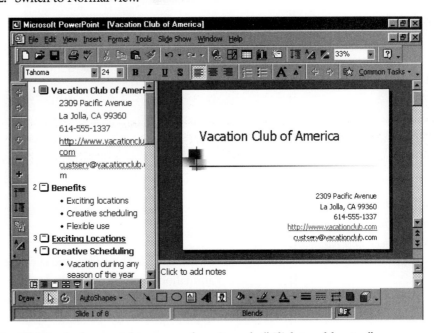

3. Click in the lower-right corner where it reads, "Click to add notes."

4. Type "Welcome the audience and thank them for coming."

5. Go to Slide 3.

6. Repeat step 3 and type "These are just a few of the thousands of resort destinations available to Vacation Club of America members."

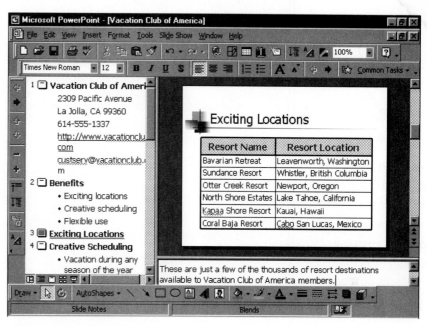

7. Go to Slide 8.

8. Repeat Step 3 and type "Ask the audience to write down these numbers and close with a joke."

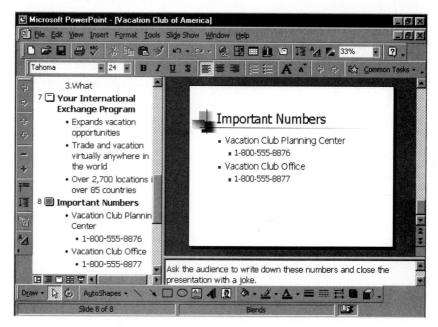

9. Save the presentation.

10. Switch to Slide Show view and view the presentation in its entirety. Notice that the notes you added do not appear in this view.

11. Choose File>Print from the Menu bar.

12. Choose Notes Pages from the Print What drop-down list box at the Print dialog box.

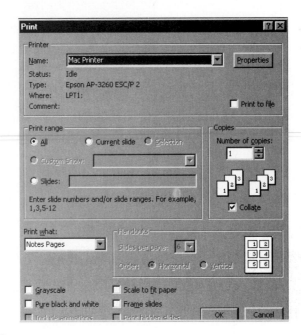

To quickly save your presentation as you are working on it, use Control-S. You should get in the habit of doing this every few minutes.

13. Click OK.

14. Save your presentation.

15. Close your presentation and exit PowerPoint.

Complete Project E: Wildflower Spas

PRESENTING ON THE WEB

CHAPTER OBJECTIVES:

To learn how to create PowerPoint presentations that can be viewed and delivered via the World Wide Web. To become familiar with the links that allow users to click on hypertext or hypermedia and be transported to another Web page. In Chapter 7 you will:

- Learn to save a PowerPoint presentation as a Web page for distribution on the World Wide Web.

- Develop an understanding of how to view a PowerPoint presentation in a Web browser.

- Learn how to view the HTML tags or source code that your Web browser is interpreting.

- Understand how to add a design template to a PowerPoint Web page.

- Learn that any media element on a slide can be used as a hyperlink to a different slide within your presentation, to an entirely different presentation, or to any existing Web site.

- Develop an understanding of how to add, edit, copy, paste, insert, and test hyperlinks.

- Learn how to set a hyperlink to an e-mail address.

- Develop an understanding of how to make your Web site available to the Internet community.

PROJECTS TO BE COMPLETED:

- The Backcountry Almanac
- Fitness Facts
- Mastering Golf
- Easy & Elegant Baking
- Wildflower Spas
- **Washington Apples Online**
- Yard Debris Recycling Program

Presenting on the Web

The World Wide Web, or simply the Web, is a component of the Internet that is based on hyperlinks. Hyperlinks allow Web developers to cross-reference Web pages by setting up links from text or other media elements such as graphics and animation. These links allow users to click on hypertext or other hypermedia and be transported to another Web page located on the same server or an entirely different server.

All Web pages, regardless of how they are created, are based on the HyperText Markup Language or HTML. HTML is a scripting language that uses specific tags that tell browsers such as Netscape Navigator and Internet Explorer how to display a document.

Save as Web Page

Because the Web has become such a huge and viable means of distributing information, PowerPoint includes an option which allows you to easily save your presentations in an HTML format so that they can be distributed via the Web. To save your presentation as an HTML document, simply choose File>Save as Web Page and PowerPoint will convert your existing presentation to HTML.

Saving a PowerPoint Presentation as a Web Page

1. Start the PowerPoint application.

2. Choose Open an existing presentation and navigate to the **SF-PowerPoint** folder. Double-click on the **Computer Viruses** file to open it.

3. Choose File>Save as Web Page.

If you don't see the Save as Web Page option, point to the double chevron at the bottom of the menu.

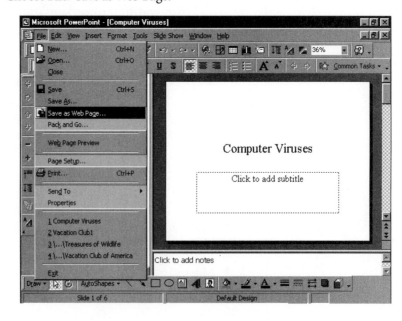

4. Perform a Save as, and save the file as "Computer Viruses 2" into your **Work in Progress** folder. Be certain that the Save as type option is set to Web Page.

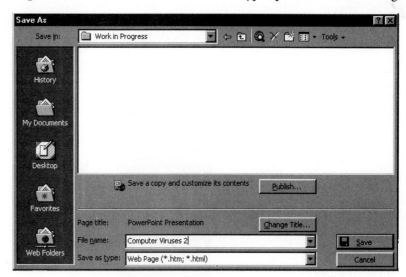

5. Close the **Computer Viruses 2** file and exit the PowerPoint application.

Opening a Presentation in a Web Browser

When you save your presentation as a Web page, PowerPoint inserts the necessary HTML tags so that the presentation can now be viewed in a Web browser. This means that in addition to opening and viewing your presentation in PowerPoint, you can now open and view your presentation in Netscape Navigator, Internet Explorer, or any other graphical-based Web browser.

The following instructions may vary slightly depending on which browser you will be using to view your Web page.

1. Start your Web browser.

2. Choose File>Open or File>Open Page.

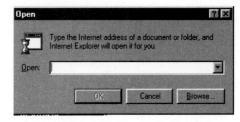

3. Choose Browse or Open File and navigate to the **Work in Progress** folder. Click on **Computer Viruses 2**.

You do not need Internet access to view your Web page from a local drive such as your hard drive or your floppy disk drive. You do need a Web browser such as Internet Explorer or Netscape Navigator. If your computer tries to make an Internet connection when you start your browser, choose Stop.

Your PowerPoint presentation may look slightly different than the one shown. This difference could be the result of the specific browser or version of browser you are using as well as the type of monitor and settings specific to your setup. Don't worry if your browser isn't displaying exactly what you see in the figure. Continue with the steps as instructed.

Some older browsers do not support the frames that are shown at the left. If you are using an older version of a browser you may not be able to complete the steps exactly as instructed.

4. Choose OK or Open until the PowerPoint presentation appears in your browser as shown.

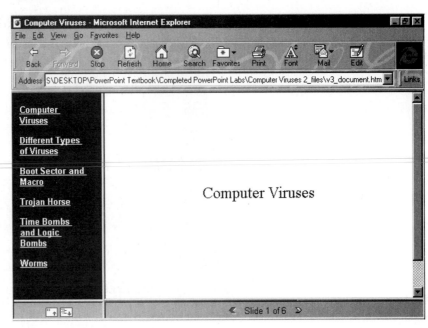

In the conversion process, PowerPoint generates a table of contents with hyperlinks that appear in the frame at the left. When you click on any of the underlined options at the left, you will be linked to the slide, which is now a separate Web page that contains the requested information. This table of contents with hyperlinks to each slide in the presentation allows users to navigate your presentation in a nonlinear manner. In other words, users do not have to view your presentation in a set order but can randomly choose to view any slide in any order.

5. Click on each of the options at the left and notice how the contents in the frame on the right side of the screen changes.

6. Click back on Computer Viruses in the left frame to return to Slide 1 or the Home page of this Web site.

7. Leave this Web Page open in your browser for the next exercise.

Viewing HTML Source Code

To get an idea of how your browser is displaying this Web page, let's take a look at the HTML tags or source code that your browser is interpreting.

1. Choose View>Source or View>Page Source from the Menu bar.

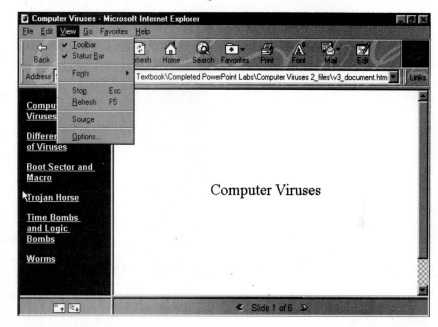

Don't worry if your HTML source code isn't exactly identical to the code shown.

The HTML tags or source code that is being interpreted by your browser should display as shown.

```
<html xmlns:o="urn:schemas-microsoft-com:office:office"
xmlns="http://www.w3.org/TR/REC-html40">

<head>
<meta http-equiv=Content-Type content="text/html; charset=windows-1252">
<meta name=ProgId content=PowerPoint.Slide>
<meta name=Generator content="Microsoft PowerPoint 9">
<link id=Main-File rel=Main-File href="Computer%20Viruses%202.htm">
<link rel=File-List href="./Computer%20Viruses%202_files/filelist.xml">
<link rel=Preview href="./Computer%20Viruses%202_files/preview.wmf">
<title>Computer Viruses</title>
<!--[if gte mso 9]><xml>
 <o:DocumentProperties>
  <o:Author>Barclay</o:Author>
  <o:LastAuthor>Barclay</o:LastAuthor>
  <o:Revision>1</o:Revision>
  <o:TotalTime>29</o:TotalTime>
  <o:Created>1999-07-05T22:57:56Z</o:Created>
  <o:LastSaved>1999-07-05T23:28:56Z</o:LastSaved>
  <o:Words>18</o:Words>
  <o:PresentationFormat>On-screen Show</o:PresentationFormat>
  <o:Bytes>6515</o:Bytes>
  <o:Paragraphs>6</o:Paragraphs>
  <o:Slides>6</o:Slides>
  <o:Version>9.2720</o:Version>
 </o:DocumentProperties>
</xml><![endif]-->
```

2. Close the HTML source code and return to your browser.

3. Close your browser.

Adding a Design Template to a Web Presentation

1. Start the PowerPoint application.

2. Choose File>Open.

3. Navigate to the **Work in Progress** folder. Click on the drop-down list box next to Files of type and choose Web Pages.

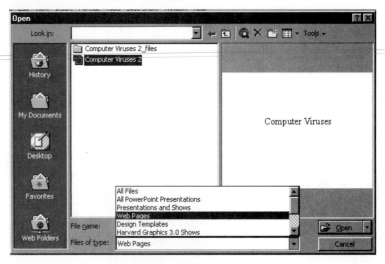

4. Click on **Computer Viruses 2** and choose Open.

5. Click on the Common Tasks drop-down list box and choose Apply Design Template.

6. Click on the Sumi Painting design template and choose Apply.

If you can't find the Sumi Painting design template, choose a different design template.

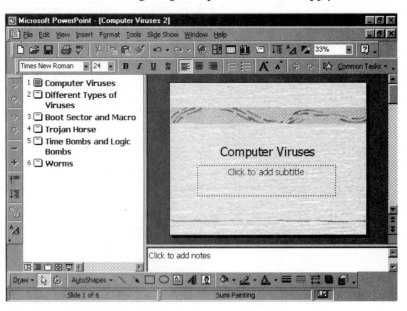

7. Save your presentation and leave it open for the next exercises.

Adding Content to Slides

1. Go to Slide 1. Type your name in the subtitle placeholder that reads "click to add subtitle."

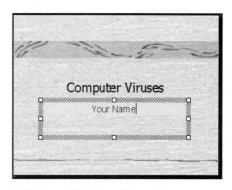

2. Go to Slide 3 and add the text shown.

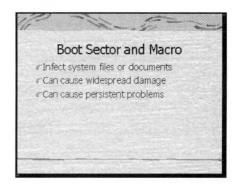

3. Complete Slides 4-6 as shown and then Save your presentation.

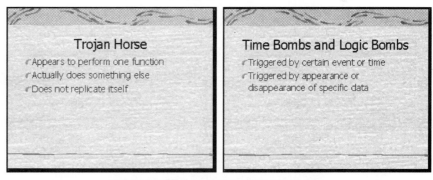

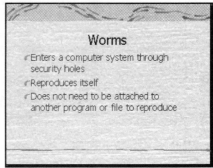

Hyperlinks

Any media element on a slide can be used as a hyperlink to a different slide within the same presentation, to an entirely different presentation, or to any existing Web site. In the broadest sense, when a media element is used as a hyperlink, it is considered hypermedia. More specifically, when text is used as a hyperlink, it is called hypertext, whereas a graphic used as a hyperlink is called a hypergraphic.

Hyperlinks allow users to navigate a presentation in a nonlinear manner. In addition, they allow users access to information that may not be part of the immediate presentation. Hyperlinks can be inserted into any PowerPoint presentation, however, they are probably most often found within presentations that will be delivered online. This ability to cross-reference or cross-link information is the foundation of the Web, and it is this feature that has made the Web an incredibly appealing tool. PowerPoint has become a useful and powerful tool for creating Web sites due to its ability to easily insert hyperlinks.

Adding a hyperlink to a presentation is simple. Select the text or object that you want to use as a hyperlink and choose Insert>Hyperlink from the Menu bar or click on the Insert Hyperlink button 🔲 on the Standard toolbar and enter the slide, presentation, or Web address you want to cross-reference.

Creating Objects to be Used as Hyperlinks

1. Go to Slide 2.

2. Click on the AutoShapes drop-down list box on the Drawing toolbar.

3. Point to Flowchart and choose Punched Tape (fourth option, fourth row).

To insert a hyperlink using a keyboard shortcut, select the text or objects you want to serve as the hyperlink and press Control-K.

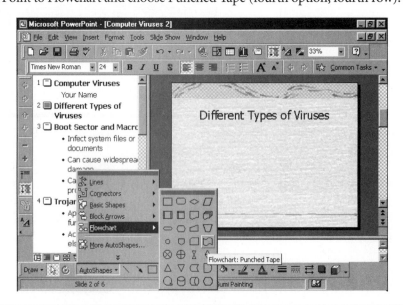

4. Position the crosshair below the "D" in Different and drag to create the shape shown.

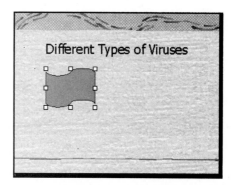

5. With the shape still selected (selection or sizing handles should appear around all sides), hold down the Control key as you drag the shape to the right.

6. Release the mouse button and choose Copy here.

7. Repeat steps 5 and 6 to create the four shapes shown.

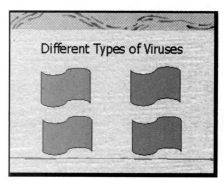

8. Save your presentation.

9. Choose the Text Box tool on the Drawing toolbar.

10. Position the crosshair inside the first shape and drag to draw a text box as shown.

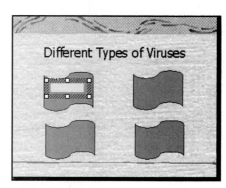

Holding down the Shift key helps ensure that the shapes and objects you draw or resize remain in proportion. You can also use the Shift key to constrain the movement and keep an object vertically or horizontally aligned when you move or copy it.

Another way to copy the object is to select it and choose Edit>Copy and then Edit>Paste from the Menu bar. The keyboard shortcuts for copy and paste are Control-C and Control-V.

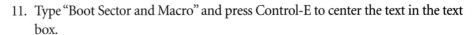

Use the selection or sizing handles to resize your text boxes as needed. Remember, when the mouse changes to a double-headed arrow you can resize an object. When the mouse changes to a four-headed arrow you can move an object.

11. Type "Boot Sector and Macro" and press Control-E to center the text in the text box.

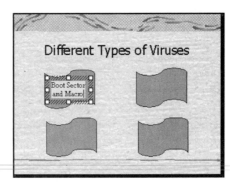

12. Repeat steps 9-11 to create the text boxes shown.

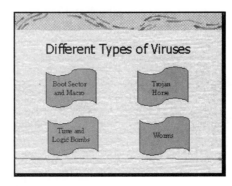

13. Hold down the Shift key and click to select each of the AutoShapes (do not select the text boxes).

14. Click on the Fill Color drop-down list box on the Drawing toolbar.

15. Choose Follow Accent Scheme Color (sixth option).

You can also double-click on a selected object(s) to get to the Format AutoShape or Object dialog box. From here you can make a variety of formatting changes including changing the fill color.

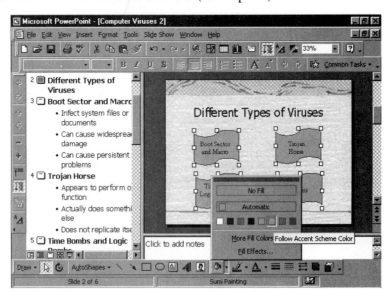

16. Save your presentation.

If you accidentally select the text box, hold down the Shift key and click on the border of the text box to deselect it.

Inserting Hyperlinks

1. Click on the first AutoShape created on Slide 2.

2. Choose Insert>Hyperlink from the Menu bar.

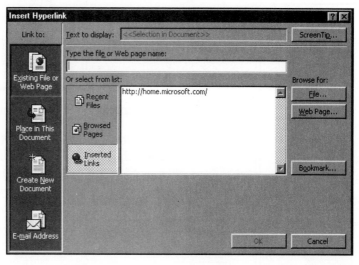

3. Choose Place in This Document under Link to: at the Insert Hyperlink dialog box.

4. Choose 3. Boot Sector and Macro under Select a place in this document.

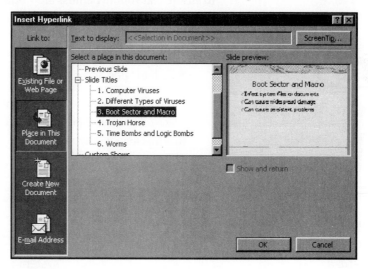

5. Choose OK.

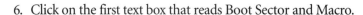

6. Click on the first text box that reads Boot Sector and Macro.

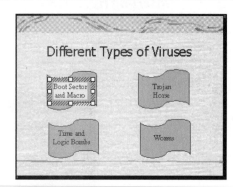

7. Repeat steps 2-5 to link the text box to Slide 3.

8. Repeats steps 1-7 to assign appropriate hyperlinks to the AutoShape and text box of each object. Be certain to link the Trojan Horse shape and text box to Slide 4, the Time and Logic Bombs shape and text box to Slide 5, and the Worms shape and text box to Slide 6.

9. Save your presentation.

Testing Hyperlinks

To ensure that your hyperlinks are working properly, you should check your hyperlinks in both PowerPoint as well as in your browser if you are creating a Web page.

1. Go to Slide 1.

2. Switch to Slide Show view.

3. From Slide 2, point to the first AutoShape and text box for Boot Sector and Macro. The mouse pointer should change to a pointing finger. This indicates that this item is a hyperlink.

4. Click the mouse button to go to Slide 3, the Boot Sector and Macro Slide.

To work properly, both the text box and the object have to be set as a hyperlink. Otherwise, it is possible that the user will try to click on one or the other and nothing will happen.

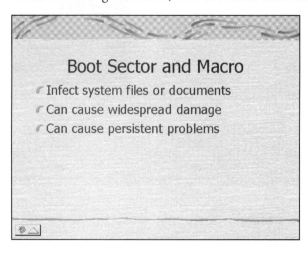

5. Press the Left Arrow key to return to Slide 2.

6. Click the Trojan Horse object to link to the Trojan Horse Slide.

7. Press the Left Arrow key twice to return to Slide 2.

8. Click on each object to test each of the hyperlinks you created on Slide 2. Press the Left Arrow key to return to Slide 2.

9. Start your browser (Internet Explorer or Netscape Navigator).

10. Choose File>Open or File>Open Page and Browse. Click **Computer Viruses2** and choose Open>OK.

11. Go to Slide 2.

If your hyperlinks don't work, switch back to Normal View, select the object or text box, choose Insert>Hyperlink, and choose the appropriate slide.

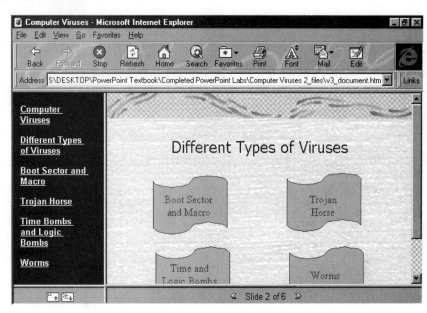

12. Click on the Boot Sector and Macro object to test the first hyperlink.

13. Choose Back to return to Slide 2.

14. Repeat steps 12 and 13 to test each of the hyperlinks on Slide 2.

15. Close your browser.

Adding Web Address Hyperlinks

Just as you can easily establish a hyperlink to a slide within a presentation, you can also create a link to any Web address by specifying the address or uniform resource locator (URL) of the Web site.

1. In PowerPoint, go to Slide 6.

2. Choose New Slide from the Common Tasks drop-down list box.

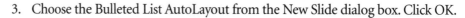

3. Choose the Bulleted List AutoLayout from the New Slide dialog box. Click OK.

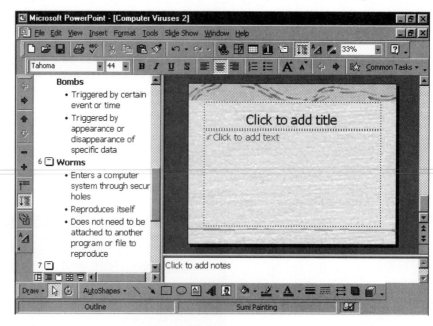

4. Click on the title placeholder to add the title "Detection and Protection".

5. Click on the bulleted list placeholder to add the text shown.

6. Select the first bulleted item.

7. Choose Insert>Hyperlink.

8. Click on Existing File or Web Page under Link to: at the Insert Hyperlink dialog box.

The shortcut to insert a new slide is Control-M.

9. Type "http://www.symantec.com" in the Type the file or Web page name: text box.

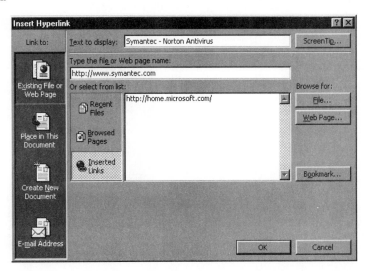

10. Click OK.

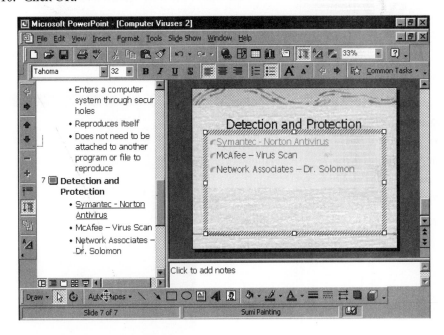

The text should appear underlined and blue. These changes indicate that a hyperlink has been applied to the text. Next, you'll make the other two bulleted items hyperlinks and then test the links you've inserted.

11. Select the second bulleted item.

12. Click on the Insert Hyperlink button  on the Standard toolbar.

To insert a hyperlink, you can also click on the Insert Hyperlink button on the Standard toolbar or press Control-K.

13. Type "http://www.mcafee.com" in the Type the file or Web page name: text box and click OK.

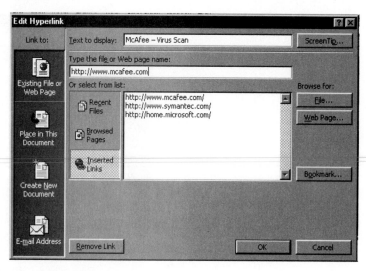

14. Select the third bulleted item.

15. Press Control-K.

16. Type "http://www.solomon.com" in the Type the file or Web page name: text box and click OK.

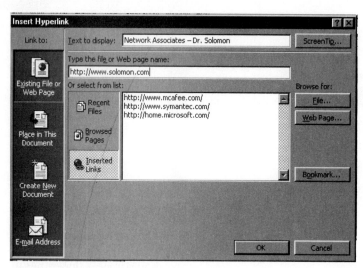

17. Save your presentation.

http stands for Hypertext Transfer Protocol. This protocol indicates to the browser that the link is going to an external Web page.

Editing Hyperlinks

The Web is not static. In this constantly changing Internet environment, you may need to modify the hyperlinks that you have set to Web addresses that have changed. In addition, you may have made a mistake when you initially set the link. PowerPoint makes it easy for you to edit your hyperlinks so that you do not need to recreate them.

1. Go to Slide 7, which is the last slide in your presentation.

2. Right-click on the last bulleted item, Network Associates - Dr. Solomon. A shortcut menu should appear as shown.

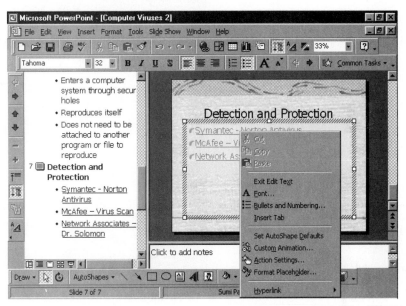

3. Choose Hyperlink>Edit Hyperlink from this shortcut menu.

4. At the Edit Hyperlink dialog box, change the address from http:// www.solomon.com to http://www.nia.com and click OK.

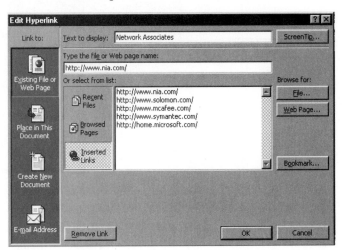

5. Save your presentation.

Pasting as Hyperlink

Though inserting a hyperlink is a simple task, copying an existing element such as text or a graphic and pasting it as a hyperlink may be even easier because the link is automatically created for you.

1. Go to Slide 1 of your presentation and switch to Slide view.

2. Select the title, Computer Viruses, and choose Edit>Copy from the Menu bar.

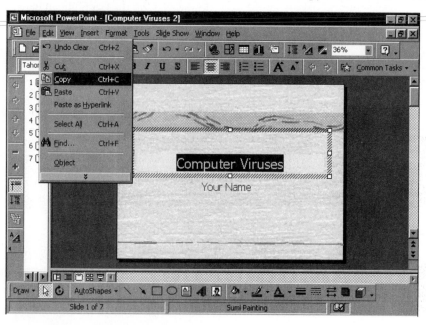

3. Go to Slide 7.

4. Click on the Text Box tool 🗎 on the Drawing toolbar and draw a text box in the lower-right corner as shown.

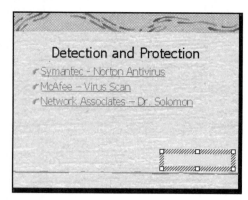

5. With the insertion point inside the text box, choose Edit>Paste as Hyperlink.

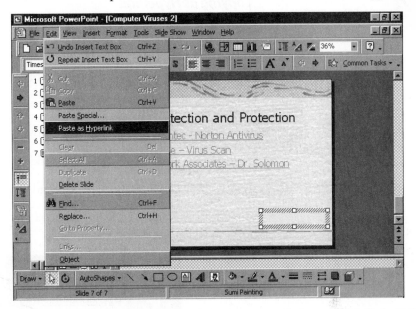

The keyboard shortcut for copy is Control-C, or you can also use the copy button on the Standard toolbar to copy a selection.

6. Right-click on the hypertext, Computer Viruses, and choose Hyperlink>Edit Hyperlink from the shortcut menu that appears.

7. Type Return to Home in the text box next to Text to display: in the Edit Hyperlink dialog box.

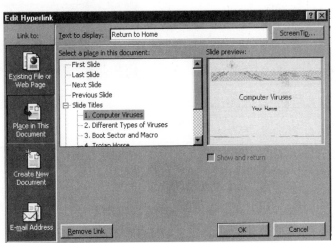

8. Choose OK and Save your presentation.

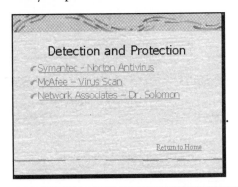

Copying as Hyperlink

1. Go to Slide 2.

2. Select the title, Different Types of Viruses, and choose Edit>Copy.

3. Go to Slide 3.

4. Create another text box in the lower-right corner of the slide.

5. Choose Edit>Paste as Hyperlink.

6. Right-click on the hyperlink and choose Hyperlink>Edit Hyperlink.

7. Type Return to Menu in the text box next to Text to display: in the Edit Hyperlink dialog box.

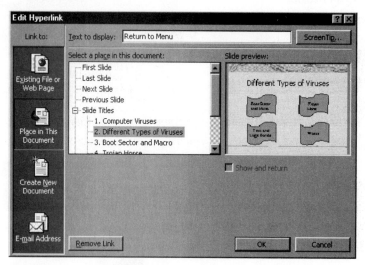

8. Choose OK.

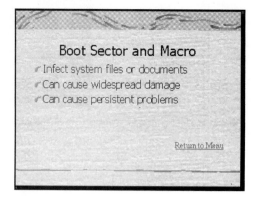

9. Save your presentation.

10. Click on the border of the text box that reads Return to Menu to select the text box.

11. Choose Edit>Copy.

12. Go to Slide 4 and choose Edit>Paste.

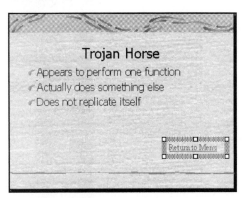

13. Go to Slide 5 and 6 and paste a copy of the Return to Menu link on each of these slides. If necessary, reposition the pasted links in the lower-right corner of the slide.

14. Save your presentation.

Adding E-mail Addresses

In addition to setting up hyperlinks to slides, other presentations, and Web addresses, you can also set a hyperlink to an e-mail address. Provided the user's browser has been properly configured, setting a hyperlink to an e-mail address will enable users to send e-mail messages directly from a Web page.

1. Go to Slide 1.

2. Type your e-mail address under your name.

3. Select your e-mail address and choose Insert>Hyperlink.

4. Click on the E-mail Address icon under the Link to: option.

5. Type your e-mail address in the text box as shown. The word mailto: will automatically be inserted before your e-mail address. Mailto: is the HTML tag the browser uses to recognize e-mail addresses.

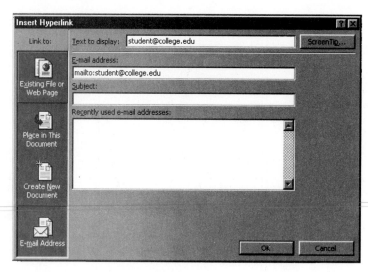

6. Choose OK.

7. Save your presentation.

A selected text box will have a dotted border. If the border of the text box appears with hashed or diagonal lines instead of dots, click on the border a second time to select it so that it appears as shown.

Testing Hyperlinks

You can test some of your hyperlinks from Slide Show view. However, in order to test hyperlinks set to e-mail addresses or external Web addresses you must use your browser and have an Internet connection.

1. In PowerPoint, go to Slide 1.

2. Switch to Slide Show view.

3. Test the internal links on Slide 2 as well as the Return to Menu and Return to Home hyperlinks on Slides 3-7.

4. Start your browser.

5. Choose File>Open or File>Open Page depending on whether you are using Internet Explorer or Netscape Navigator.

Be sure to click on the Computer Viruses2 file, not the folder.

6. Choose Browse and click on **Computer Viruses 2.**

7. Choose Open and OK to open this Web page in your browser.

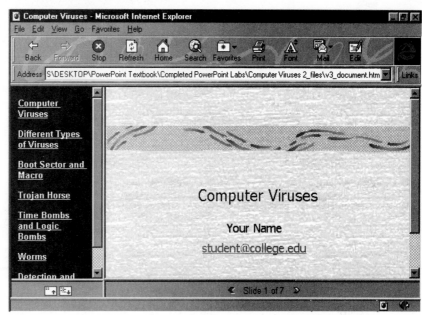

8. Click on the e-mail address under your name.

9. If the browser has been properly configured, an e-mail window should display. Send yourself an e-mail message.

10. Click on Different Types of Viruses in the left frame.

11. Click on the Boot Sector and Macro object in the right frame to test the link.

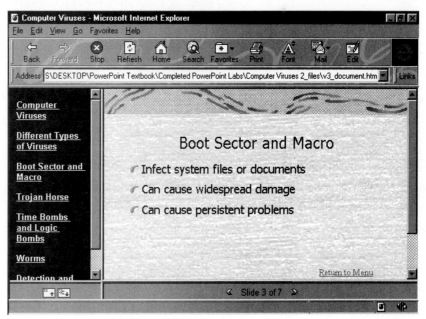

12. Click the Return to Menu hyperlink in the lower-right corner to test the link back to Slide 2.

If an e-mail window does not display, your browser may not be properly configured.

There are several reasons why external links may not work. If your links do not work, check to be certain that you have typed in the correct Web address or URL. You can do this by pointing to the link and looking in the status bar at the bottom of the browser. If the address is incorrect, return to PowerPoint, right-click on the link and choose Hyperlink>Edit Hyperlink.

In addition to typing in the incorrect Web address, your hyperlink may not work because Web addresses change and servers can be busy or unavailable. If you have typed in the correct address and you still can't access the Web site, try again later or contact technical support.

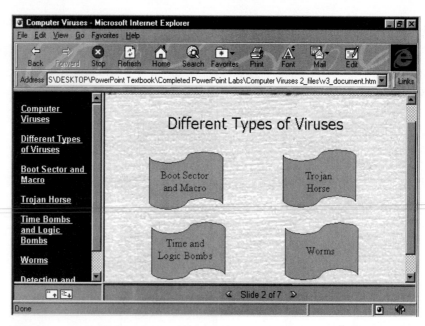

13. Repeat steps 11 and 12 to test the hyperlinks for the other three objects on Slide 2.

14. Go to Slide 7, Detection and Protection.

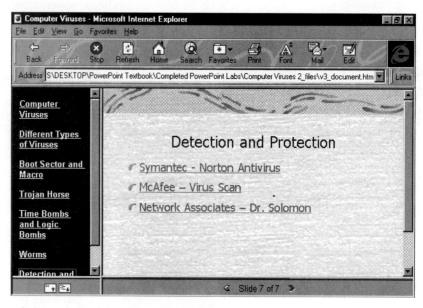

15. Click on each of the external hyperlinks to Symantec, McAfee, and Network Associates to test these links.

16. Finally, click on the Return to Home link to ensure that this final link takes you back to Slide 1, which is the home page of this Web site.

17. Close your browser.

18. Return to PowerPoint and make any necessary changes.

19. Save your presentation.

Publishing Your Presentation to the Web

At this time, the Web site you have just created is only available from your local hard drive or floppy disk. In other words, you are the only person who has access to this Web site. If you want to make this Web site available to the rest of the Internet community, you must first upload all of the files associated with this Web site to a server that is accessible by all users surfing the Web.

Most Internet Service Providers (ISPs) allocate a set amount of disk space on a file server for posting Web pages. This benefit is generally included to their subscribers as part of the monthly fee paid for Internet access. In addition, there are sites that allow you to post your Web site for free if you don't have an ISP. Generally, these services require you to include advertising banners on your Web site.

To actually publish or upload your Web site to a file server, you must first contact your Internet Service Provider or one of the free services mentioned above to obtain instructions and details on where and how to post your site. Once you have obtained these details, you can follow the instructions below to publish your page.

Publishing Web Pages

1. Choose File>Save as Web Page from the Menu bar.

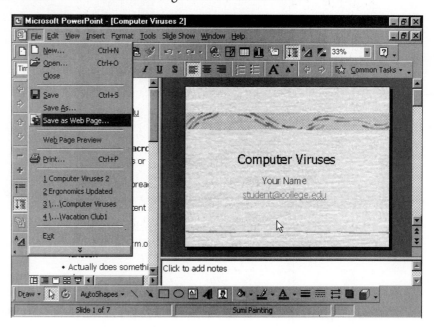

2. Click on the Publish button next to Save a copy and customize its contents in the middle of the Save As dialog box.

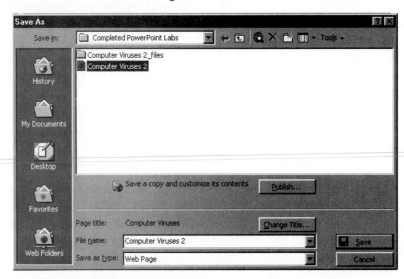

3. At the Publish as Web Page dialog box, you'll need to specify the path and file name designated by your Internet Service Provider.

4. Choose Publish.

5. Exit PowerPoint.

Complete Project F: Washington Apples Online

CHAPTER 8

DELIVERING YOUR PRESENTATION

CHAPTER OBJECTIVE:

To learn about many of PowerPoint's delivery and output techniques that will enhance your presentation and make you a more effective presenter. In Chapter 8 you will:

- Learn how to add speaker notes to your presentation.

- Develop an understanding of how to add transitions and animation to your presentation.

- Learn how to start your slide show on any slide.

- Use PowerPoint's on-screen navigation tools to navigate nonlinearly.

- Use the Pen tool during a presentation to write on a slide just as you would write on a whiteboard. You will also learn how to change pointer options, and change the screen during a presentation.

- Preview a presentation in black-and-white to determine how it will look when printed.

- Learn how to print slides, audience handouts, outlines, and speaker notes.

PROJECTS TO BE COMPLETED:

- The Backcountry Almanac
- Fitness Facts
- Mastering Golf
- Easy & Elegant Baking
- Wildflower Spas
- Washington Apples Online
- **Yard Debris Recycling Program**

Delivering Your Presentation

In addition to helping you organize your thoughts and create attractive visual aids for both you and your audience, PowerPoint also offers various slide show tools that will enhance the effectiveness of your delivery. In addition to delivering your presentation on-screen, you may want or need to prepare transparencies for an overhead projector or provide your audience with a hard copy of your presentation. PowerPoint offers extensive print options that will allow you to accomplish these tasks as well as prepare printed copies of speakers notes for yourself.

Adding Speaker Notes

1. Start the PowerPoint application.

2. Choose Open an existing presentation. Navigate to the **SF-PowerPoint** folder and double-click on the **Emergencies** file to open it.

3. Go to Slide 2.

4. Choose View>Notes Page.

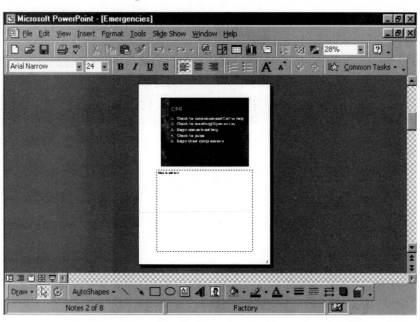

If you wish to zoom to a percentage that is not listed in the Zoom drop-down list box, type the number in the Zoom text box and press Enter.

5. Click on the drop-down list box next to Zoom on the Standard toolbar and choose 66%.

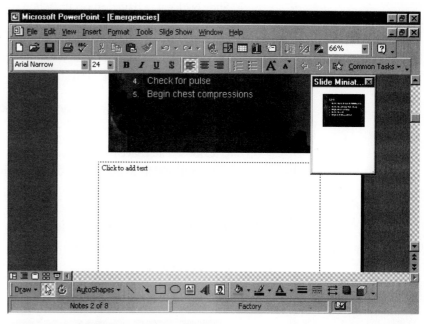

6. Click in the placeholder and add the following text in the Notes area of the page: "Think ABC - Airway, Breathing, Circulation".

Keep your presentation notes short and concise so that you aren't tempted to read to the audience as you deliver your presentation.

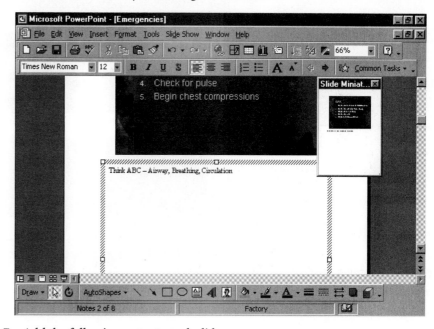

7. Add the following notes to each slide:

Slide 3: "If the person is conscious, ask them if they are choking".

Slide 4: "Provide information - substance taken, how much, when, age, and health status of poisoned individual."

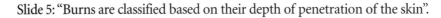

Slide 5: "Burns are classified based on their depth of penetration of the skin".

Slide 6: "Heat exhaustion occurs when the body is unable to cool off".

Slide 7: "Hypothermia is when your body temperature drops below normal and body heat is lost faster than it can be produced." "Frostbite is the freezing of the skin or tissue near the skin surface".

Slide 8: "Shock is always an emergency and requires professional medical help immediately".

8. Choose File>Save As and save the presentation as "Emergencies Updated" into your **Work in Progress** folder. Keep this file open for the following exercises.

Adding Transitions and Animation

1. Go to Slide 1.

2. Switch to Slide Sorter view.

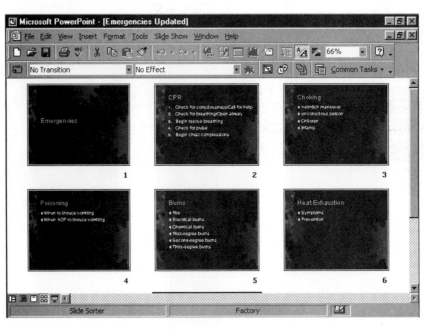

You can press Control-A to select all of the slides in your presentation.

3. Choose Edit>Select All.

4. Click on the Slide Transition Effects drop-down list box and choose Cover Left.

5. Click on the Preset Animation drop-down list box and choose Fly From Left.

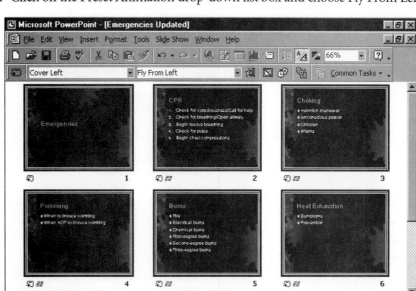

6. Click on Slide 1.

7. Switch to Slide Show view and preview your presentation in its entirety.

8. Save the presentation.

Slide Show Features

PowerPoint offers a variety of slide show tools that can be used to enhance the delivery of your presentation. PowerPoint's slide show tools can be accessed from any slide as a slide show is being delivered. To access these tools, click the right mouse button or position the mouse pointer in the lower-left corner of the slide until the icon of an outlined slide and arrow appear. Click on this icon to access the same menu options that appear if you right-click on any area of the slide.

Starting a Slide Show on Any Slide

You will generally begin a presentation by starting at Slide 1. However, there may be times when you want to start your slide show in the middle of the presentation. You do not have to begin at the beginning. When you switch to Slide Show view, your presentation will begin on whichever slide is currently the active or selected slide before switching views.

1. Switch to Slide Sorter view.

2. Click outside of the slides on the white background to deselect the slides.

3. Click on Slide 3 to select it or make it the active slide. A darker border will appear around the active slide.

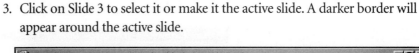

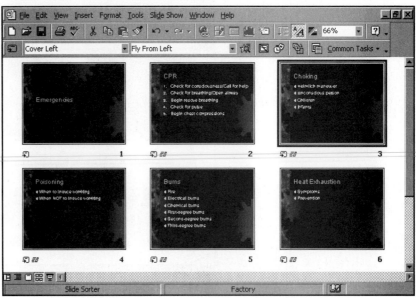

4. Switch to Slide Show view. Slide 3 should display in full screen as shown.

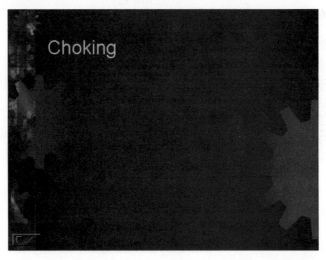

5. Click the left mouse button to view your presentation from Slide 3 or Press Esc to return to Slide Sorter view.

6. Choose View>Normal.

7. Go to Slide 6.

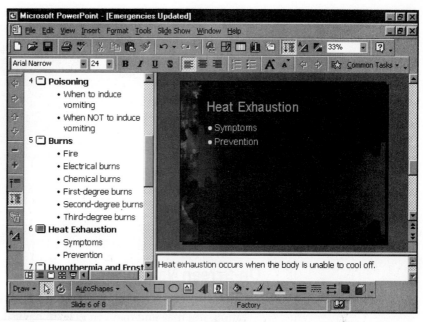

8. Switch to Slide Show view and click the left mouse button or press the Right Arrow key to view your presentation from Slide 6 to the end.

9. Switch to Outline view.

10. Click on Slide 5.

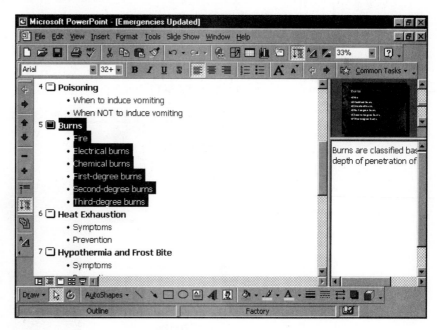

You can end a slide show at any time by right-clicking on the slide and choosing End Show.

11. Switch to Slide Show view and run your presentation from Slide 5.

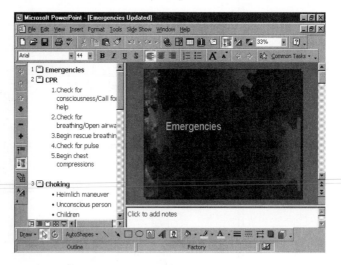

On-Screen Navigation Tools

As you begin practicing your presentation, and also while you are giving your presentation, you may find that you need to navigate nonlinearly. In other words, you may need to return to a previous slide or advance to a slide that is further along in your presentation. In PowerPoint, you can easily go to any slide in your presentation at any time during the slide show.

Navigating a Presentation

1. Switch to Normal view.

2. Go to Slide 1 of your presentation.

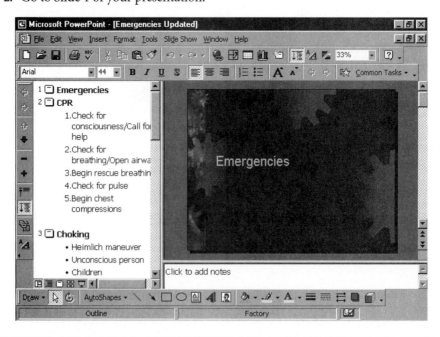

3. Switch to Slide Show view.

4. Click the left mouse button to advance to Slide 3, Choking.

5. Press the Left Arrow key to return to Slide 2, CPR.

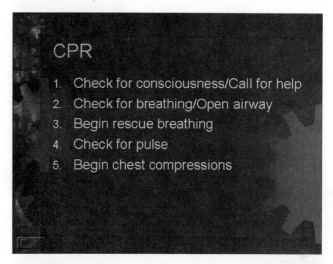

6. Press the Left Arrow key again. The fifth bulleted item should disappear.

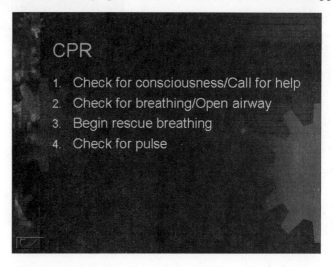

Remember, you can also press the Right Arrow key to advance to the next bulleted item or slide.

If you have applied animation to slides, the Left Arrow key will take you back one step at a time. One step may be back one slide or back one bulleted item. For this reason, using the shortcut menu to navigate your presentation may be more efficient than using the Left Arrow key. In addition to going to the next and previous slides, from the Shortcut menu you can use the Go command to immediately navigate to any slide in the presentation.

7. Right-click anywhere on the slide to bring up the Shortcut menu.

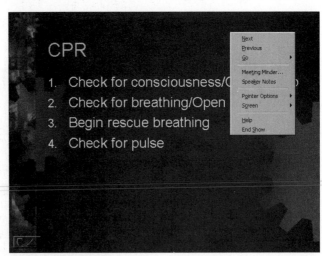

8. Point to Go on the Shortcut menu.

9. Choose Slide Navigator.

Right-clicking and using the Shortcut menu to navigate from slide to slide is often the most efficient method.

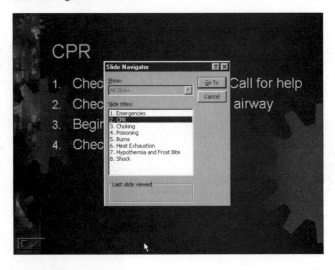

10. Click on Slide 7, Hypothermia and Frost Bite, and choose Go To.

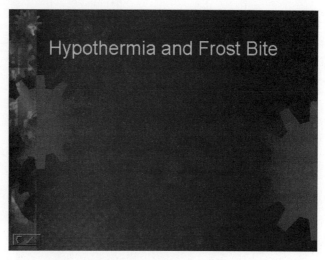

11. Right-click anywhere on Slide 7.

12. Choose Go>Previously Viewed to return to Slide 2, CPR.

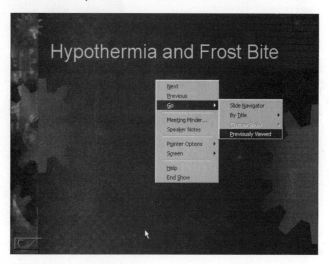

13. Right-click anywhere on Slide 2.

14. Choose Go>By Title>5 Burns to quickly move to Slide 5, Burns.

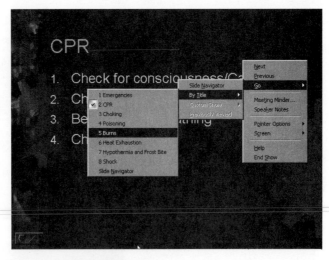

15. Right-click anywhere on Slide 5.

16. Choose Previous to return to Slide 4.

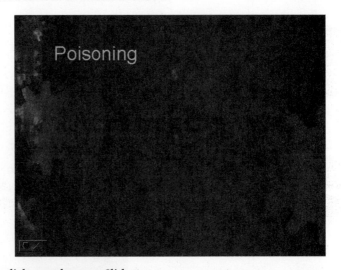

17. Right-click anywhere on Slide 4.

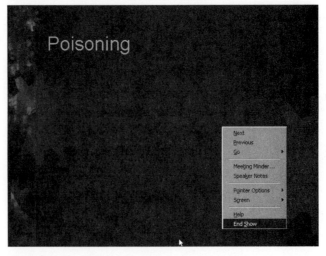

18. Choose End Show to return to Normal view.

Additional Slide Show Features

In addition to navigating to any slide at any time, PowerPoint includes features such as a pen that allows you to write on the slide during your presentation as well as the option to display a blank screen at any time.

Using the Pen Tool

The Pen tool is used to write on a slide just as you would write on a chalkboard, whiteboard, or overhead transparency. Though the Pen tool is not very useful for writing text, you can use it to draw circles or underlines to emphasize important points and arrows or lines to identify relationships. The drawings created by the Pen tool during a presentation are not permanent. As soon as you move to the next slide or next bulleted item, anything created with the Pen tool will disappear.

1. Go to Slide 1 of your presentation.

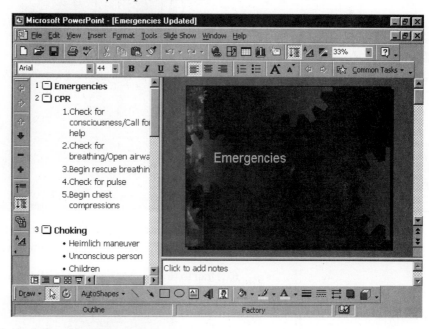

2. Switch to Slide Show view.

3. Click the left mouse button twice to navigate to the first bulleted item of Slide 2.

You can end a slide show at any time by pressing the Esc key.

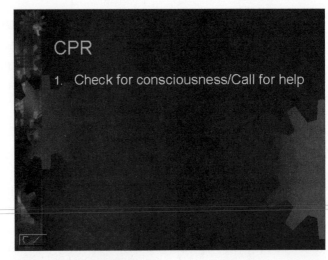

4. Right-click anywhere on Slide 2.

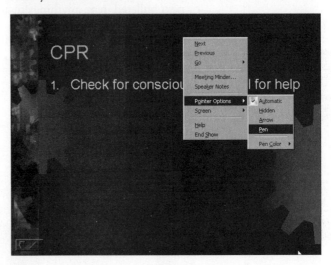

5. Choose Pointer Options>Pen from the Shortcut menu. The shape of your mouse should change from a pointer to a pen.

6. Drag to draw a circle around "Call for help" in the first bulleted item.

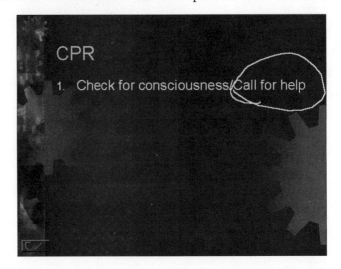

7. Right-click anywhere on Slide 2.

8. Choose Pointer Options>Automatic.

9. Click the left mouse button nine times to navigate to the last bulleted item in Slide 3.

10. Click on the icon of the slide and arrow in the lower-left corner of the screen.

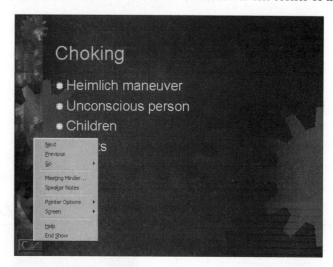

11. Choose Pointer Options>Pen.

12. Draw three underlines under "Infants."

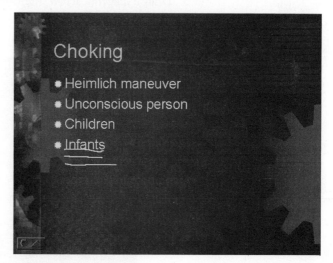

13. Click on the icon of the slide and arrow in the lower-left corner of the screen.

14. Choose Pointer Options>Arrow.

The default pen color will match the color scheme established by the selected design template.

Changing the Pen Tool Color

1. Right-click anywhere on Slide 3.

2. Choose Go>By Title>8 Shock.

3. Right-click anywhere on Slide 8.

4. Choose Pen Options>Pen Color>Magenta.

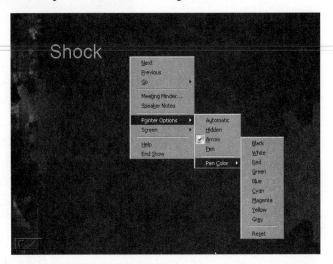

When you are finished using the Pen tool, don't forget to change the Pointer Options back to Arrow or Automatic so that you can navigate through the remainder of your presentation.

5. Draw a magenta arrow pointing to the upper-right corner of the screen to illustrate the direction that the patient's feet should be raised if he/she is in shock.

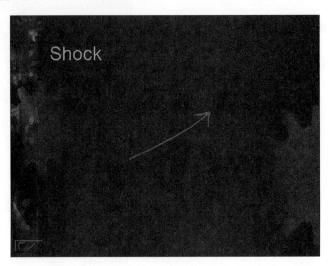

Anything written on-screen with the Pen tool will be removed as soon as you advance to the next or previous bullet or slide.

6. Click on the icon of the slide and arrow in the lower-left corner of the screen.

7. Choose Pointer Options>Pen Color>Reset.

8. Underline the word "Shock."

9. Right-click anywhere on Slide 8. Then choose Screen>Erase Pen.

Changing the Screen

Though PowerPoint slides generally add to the effectiveness of your presentation and enhance the message you are trying to deliver, there may be times when the slides become a distraction to the audience. For example, during the middle of your presentation a member of the audience may pose a question that should be further addressed. If this happens, you may wish to black the screen in order to focus on the question or concern. By hiding the slide, the audience members will not be distracted by the PowerPoint presentation. Instead, their attention will be redirected to the discussion.

1. Right-click anywhere on Slide 8.

2. Choose Pointer Options>Automatic.

3. Right-click anywhere on Slide 8.

4. Choose Go>By Title>6 Heat Exhaustion.

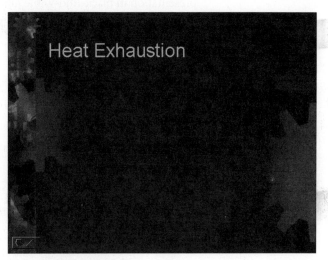

5. Right-click anywhere on Slide 6.

6. Choose Screen>Black Screen.

7. Right-click on the black screen.

8. Choose Screen>Unblack Screen.

9. Press the Esc key to return to Normal view and keep the file open.

Printing Your Presentation

Although PowerPoint slides are probably most often viewed on a computer screen, there are times when you may need or wish to print a portion or all of your presentation. For example, you may be asked to deliver a presentation in a facility that is not equipped with a computer and projection system. In this case, you could print your slides and prepare overhead transparencies from them. In addition, you may wish to print speaker notes for yourself or handouts for your audience.

If you have a color printer, your slides will be printed in the colors shown on the screen. If you have a black-and-white printer, your slides will be printed in different shades of gray.

Although clicking the Print button is the quickest way to print your presentation, if you click the Print button on the Standard toolbar, you will not be able to set any of the print options. If you want to specify what you would like to print as well as the number of copies you want printed, you should first go to the Print dialog box.

Previewing Your Presentation in Black-and-White

If you do not have a color printer, or if you plan to photocopy any of your slides, handouts, or speaker notes using a black-and-white photocopier, it is a good idea to preview your presentation in black-and-white before printing. Previewing your presentation in black-and-white allows you to determine in advance whether or not the color scheme and design template will be acceptable in black-and-white.

1. Go to Slide 1.

2. If necessary, switch to Slide view.

3. Click on the Grayscale Preview button 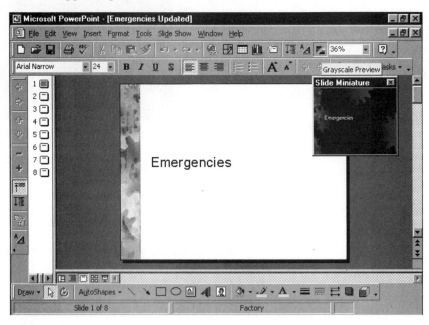 on the Standard toolbar to view Slide 1 as it will appear if printed in black-and-white.

4. Click on the Grayscale Preview button again to turn the design template colors back on.

5. Go to Slide 6.

6. Choose View>Black and White.

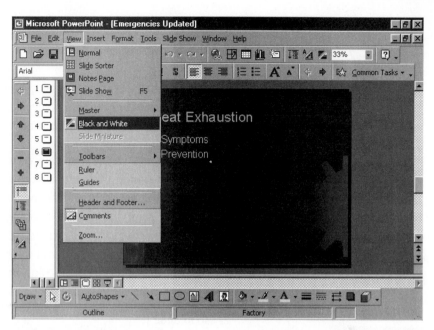

7. Choose View>Black and White a second time to turn the black-and-white preview off again.

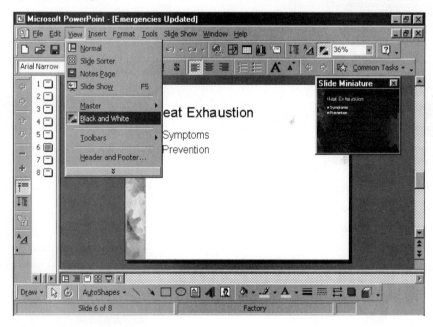

8. Save your presentation.

The keyboard shortcut that will take you to the Print dialog box so that you can set your print options is Control-P.

If you do not see the Grayscale Preview button, choose View>Toolbars and make certain that there is a check mark next to Standard. You can also choose View>Black and White from the Menu bar.

The Grayscale Preview button is considered a toggle button. If you press the button once, the feature is turned on. When you press the button a second time, the feature is turned off again.

Printing Slides

From the Print dialog box you can select a printer, make changes to the printer setup, choose a print range, select options, specify what you want to print, as well as specify the number of copies and whether or not you want the copies to be collated.

Though PowerPoint will automatically convert your color slides to shades of gray if you do not have a color printer, if you know that your final printout will be in black-and-white, you will probably get a cleaner copy if you select the black-and-white option from the Print dialog box. Therefore, if your output will be black-and-white, preview your slides in black-and-white first and then choose the Grayscale or Pure black-and-white option from the Print dialog box. You may want to print the slides in black-and-white even if you have a color printer, because printing slides in color will quickly consume the ink in your color print cartridges.

1. Go to Slide 1.

2. Choose View>Black and White.

3. Choose File>Print.

4. Put a check mark next to Pure black and white in the lower-left corner of the Print dialog box. With the exception of the printer Name, the other settings should be identical to those shown.

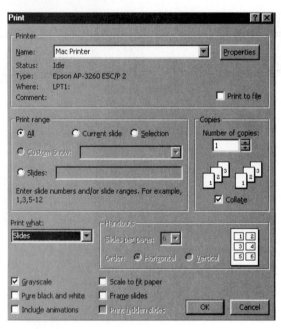

5. Choose OK to print the entire slide show.

Printing Audience Handouts

Another nice feature of PowerPoint is its ability to print audience handouts. Audience handouts allow you to print more than one slide per page. There are two schools of thought regarding when to distribute your handouts. Some presenters give the audience the handouts in advance so that the audience can take notes as the presentation is delivered. Other presenters give the handouts after the presentation has been delivered so that the audience isn't distracted.

1. Press Control-P to access the Print dialog box.

2. Choose Handouts in the drop-down list box under Print what.

3. Set the number of Slides per page to 4 under Handouts.

4. If necessary, choose the Horizontal radio button.

5. Put a check mark in the Pure black and white checkbox.

6. Set the Number of copies to 5 as shown.

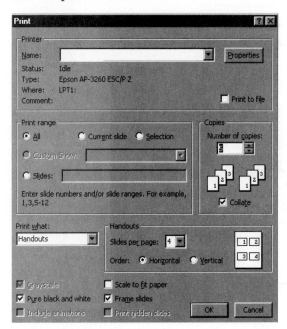

7. Choose OK to print five, collated copies of the audience handouts.

When you print a slide in PowerPoint, the default orientation is Landscape. The Landscape orientation is wider than it is tall. If you wish to change the orientation to Portrait, which is taller than it is wide, choose Properties and select the Portrait radio button under Orientation.

If you choose to print more than one copy, the Collate option specifies that the copies be collated or printed in order within a set (1-2-3-4-5, 1-2-3-4-5) rather than printing all of the copies of Slide 1 followed by all of the copies of Slide 2 and so forth. (1-1, 2-2, 3-3, 4-4, 5-5.)

Printing Outlines

Many speakers deliver their presentations from outlines or notes placed on 3 x 5" cards. Rather than having to recreate your presentation and notes in an outline or rewrite it onto 3 x 5" cards, PowerPoint allows you to print outlines and speakers notes.

1. Go to Slide 1 of your presentation.

2. Choose File>Print.

3. Choose Outline View from the Print what drop-down list box.

4. Set the number of copies to 1.

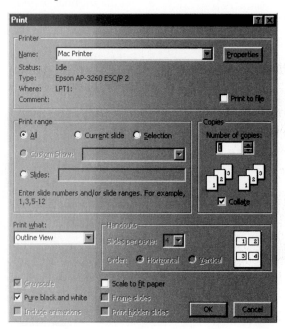

5. Click OK to print one copy of the outline.

In addition to printing all of the slides or selected slides, from the Print Range section of the Print dialog box you can also choose to print only the Current Slide, which prints the slide currently displayed on the screen or you can specify which slides to print in the Slides text box. If you use the Slides text box, you can insert a hyphen to indicate that you would like to print a range (1-5) or commas to indicate specific slides (1, 3, 5). In addition, you can combine ranges with individual slides (1-3, 5).

Printing Speaker Notes

1. Switch to Slide Sorter view.

2. Click on Slide 2 to select it. It should appear with a dark border around it.

3. Hold down the Shift key and click on Slide 8 to select all of the slides except Slide 1.

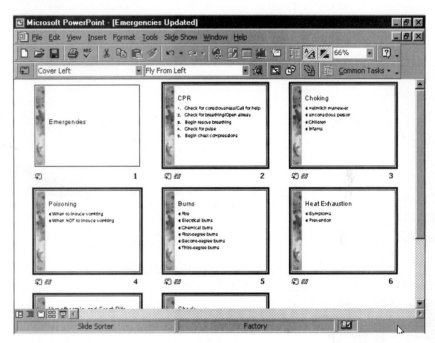

4. Choose File>Print.

5. Choose Selection under Print range to specify that you only want to print the slides that have been selected (Slides 2-8).

6. Choose Notes Pages from the Print what drop-down list box.

7. Put a check mark in the Pure black and white checkbox.

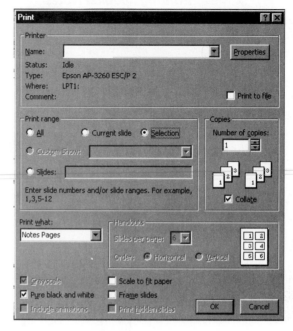

8. Click OK to print speakers notes of the selected slides (Slides 2-8).

9. Save your presentation.

10. Exit PowerPoint.

Complete Project G: Yard Debris Recycling Program

POWER POINT HELP

CHAPTER OBJECTIVE:

To learn how to use PowerPoint's built-in online Help system — one of the most efficient means of troubleshooting and productivity learning. In Chapter 9 you will:

- Become familiar with PowerPoint's Office Assistant, which is designed to provide you with an intuitive and interactive interface for receiving help on PowerPoint's features.

- Develop an understanding of Contents, which organizes online Help similar to a table of contents in a book where topics are arranged by category.

- Learn how to use the Answer Wizard which is similar to the Office Assistant.

- Develop an understanding of how to use the Index option to find an alphabetical listing of Help topics: the Index option is often the most efficient method of accessing online Help.

- Learn to use Context-Sensitive Help to click on any object on-screen to obtain information about that object.

PowerPoint Help

In addition to using textbooks to learn PowerPoint 2000, at the touch of your fingertips you can get assistance from the online help system that comes packaged with the program. Online help has improved over time, and though it may take several searches to find what you are looking for, when used properly, online help is one of the most efficient ways of troubleshooting and productively learning to use PowerPoint.

There are several different categories of online help. Each category accesses the same online help database. However, each category uses a slightly different method of searching the database.

Office Assistant

To Hide the Office Assistant, choose Help>Hide Office Assistant.

The Office Assistant is designed to provide you with an intuitive and interactive agent with whom you can interface. You ask questions of the Office Assistant in the same manner that you would ask a question of a teacher or trainer. The Office Assistant will then answer your question and provide you with step-by-step instructions on how to complete a task.

In addition to answering your questions, the Office Assistant may also offer tips or suggestions on how to more efficiently complete a task. As you are working, don't be surprised if the Office Assistant appears on your screen to offer suggestions or advice. As is true with human beings who offer unsolicited advice, at times you are probably most grateful, while at other times you may simply be annoyed. Remember that you can turn the Office Assistant off at any time.

Using the Office Assistant

1. Start PowerPoint.

2. Choose Blank Presentation and click OK.

3. Choose the Title Slide AutoLayout and click OK.

4. Choose Help>Show the Office Assistant.

The animated paperclip, ClipIt, is the default Office Assistant. However, you can choose from several different animated Office Assistants.

5. Type "How do I apply a design template?" in the Office Assistant textbox.

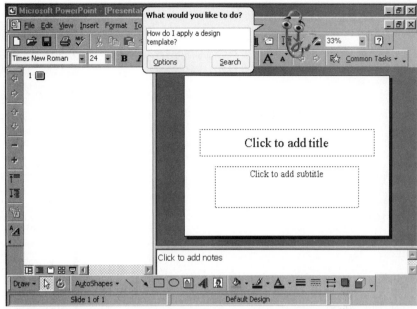

6. Choose Search.

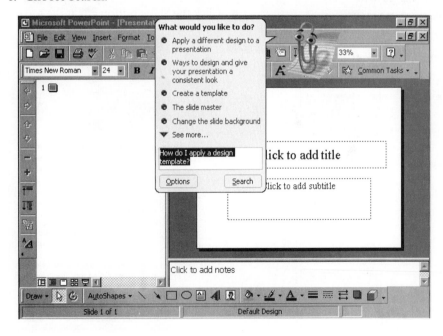

7. Click on the first blue bullet, "Apply a different design to a presentation", to see the help topic.

Options at the top of each Help topic allow you to Show Help, go to the Previous or Next Help topic, Print a Help topic, or choose from a list of options.

8. Click the Show button 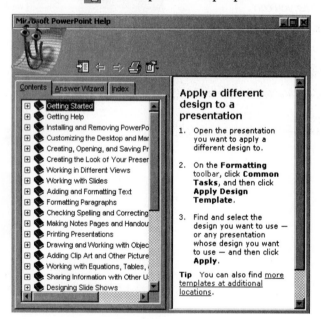 at the top of the Help topic.

9. Leave the file open for the following exercises.

F1 is the keyboard shortcut used to access online Help.

Contents

Contents organizes online Help similar to a table of contents in a book where topics are arranged or grouped together by category.

Using Contents to Access Online Help

1. Click on the Contents tab, then click the plus sign to the left of the "Working with Slides" category. This category expands and the topics within it are now visible.

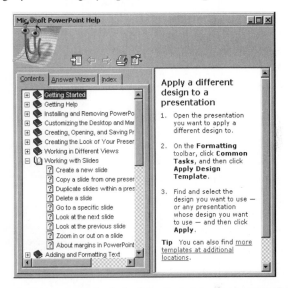

Another way to expand a category is to double-click on the topic.

2. Click on the minus sign to the left of the "Working with Slides" category to collapse or hide the topics.

3. Click on the plus sign to the left of the "Working with Slides" category to expand it again.

4. Click on "Create a new slide" to display the Help topic at the right, as shown.

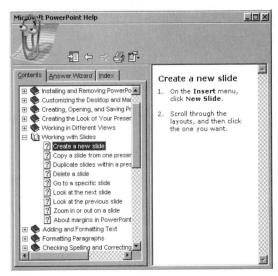

As you work, you'll notice that the animated Office Assistant continues to change shape. For example, ClipIt may rub its head to indicate that it is thinking.

The Answer Wizard

Like the Office Assistant, the Answer Wizard allows you to have a dialog.

Using the Answer Wizard to Access Online Help

1. Click on the Answer Wizard tab.

2. Type "Change the slide layout" in the text box under What would you like to do? Choose Search.

3. Click on the first option under "Select topic to display" to view the Help topic shown.

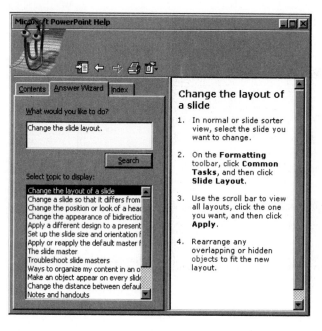

Some Help topics include a Show Me option that gives you a virtual demonstration of what to do. Other Help topics include hyperlinks that take you to cross-references that provide related assistance.

Index

The Index option under online Help is similar to using the Index at the back of a book. In the Index you will find an alphabetical listing of topics. If you know exactly what you are trying to find, Index is probably the most efficient method of accessing online Help.

Using the Index to Access Online Help

1. Click on the Index tab.

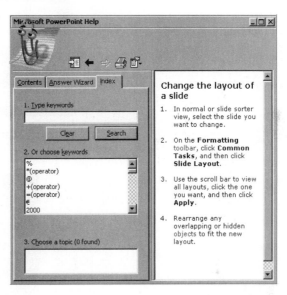

At the Index tab, you can also choose from a list of keywords.

2. Type "transition" in the first text box under Type keywords.

3. Click Search.

4. Click on "Add transitions to a slide show," the first topic under 3. Choose a topic (25 found) to display the Help topic shown.

5. Click the Show Me button. PowerPoint Help displays the Slide Transition dialog box.

6. Close the Slide Transition dialog box.

7. Close the Help dialog box.

You may also find context-sensitive help or question mark help at a dialog box. If you see a question mark to the left of the close button, you can click on the question mark and then click anywhere within the dialog box for further information.

What's This?

In addition to accessing a database of Help topics, you can also use context-sensitive Help or question mark Help. When you access context-sensitive Help your mouse shape changes to a pointer carrying a question mark. When your mouse shape appears like this, you can click on any object on the screen and get help information on whatever you click.

Using Context-Sensitive Help

1. Choose Help>What's This?

2. Click on the Save button on the Standard toolbar to display the information box.

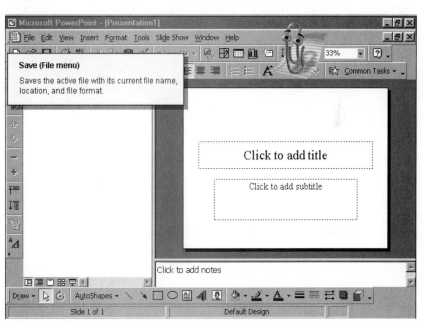

3. Click on the slide to remove the information box.

4. Choose Help>What's This?

If the mouse pointer appears with a question mark, What's This? has been activated.

What's This? is only activated for the next button, icon, or other screen element that you click. After displaying information about the item you have clicked on, it automatically turns itself off. You can toggle What's This? on and off by choosing Help>What's This? as needed.

5. Click on the Common Tasks drop-down list box and choose Slide Layout to display an information box on slide layout.

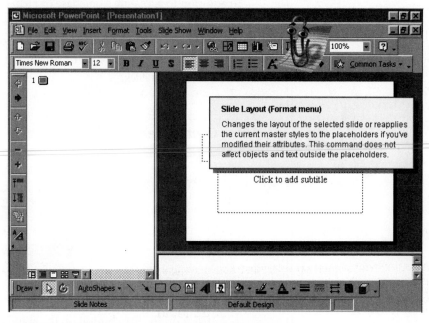

6. Click on the slide to remove the information box.

7. Exit PowerPoint. Do not save the blank presentation.

REVIEW #2

CHAPTERS 6 THROUGH 9:

In Chapters 6 through 9, you learned how to use PowerPoint's additional features to enhance you presentations. You learned how to create presentations that can be viewed and delivered via the World Wide Web, while becoming familiar with the links that allow users to click on hypertext or hypermedia and be transported to another Web page. You learned about PowerPoint's delivery and output techniques to enhance your presentation, and make you a more effective presenter. And finally, you learned how to use PowerPoint's online Help system to answer any questions you might have about the program's many features. After completing the final chapters of this course, you should:

- Understand how to create a presentation from existing slides; how to import text from word processors into your presentation; understand the importance of tables, and know how to create and modify them. You should be familiar with AutoNumber bullets; understand how to customize bullets; know how to wrap text in a text box; understand how to add slide transitions; know how to add animation to your slides; and understand how to add speaker's notes to your presentations.

- Know how to save your presentations as Web pages in an HTML format for distribution on the World Wide Web. You should understand how to view a PowerPoint presentation in a Web browser, and how to view the HTML tags or source code that your Web browser is interpreting. You should know how to add a design template to a PowerPoint Web page, and how to add content to slides. You should have learned that any media element on a slide can be used as a hyperlink to a different slide. You should understand how to add, edit, copy, paste, insert, and test hyperlinks.

- Have developed a solid understanding of how to add speaker notes, transitions, and animations to your presentations. You should know how to use the Pen tool for emphasis during a presentation. You should understand how to preview a presentation in black-and-white. And you should know how to print slides, audience handouts, outlines, and speaker notes.

- Be familiar with PowerPoint's online Help system. You should know how to use the Office Assistant; understand how Contents and Index organizes online Help; be familiar with the Answer Wizard; and finally, understand how to use Context-Sensitive Help.

Project A: The Backcountry Almanac

Create a Blank Presentation

1. Start the PowerPoint application.

2. Choose Blank presentation and click OK.

3. Choose the Title Slide AutoLayout and click OK.

4. Click to add the title "The Backcountry Almanac".

5. Click to add the subtitle and type your name.

If the Office Assistant appears on your screen, choose Help>Hide Office Assistant.

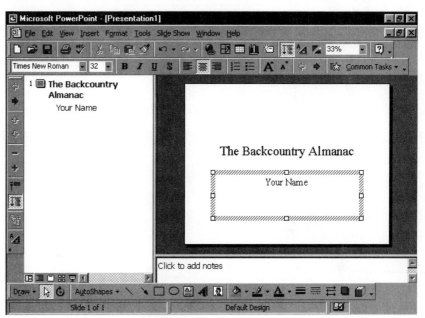

Adding Slides to a Presentation

1. Click on the Common Tasks drop-down list box.

2. Choose New Slide.

3. Click on the Bulleted List AutoLayout and choose OK.

4. Click to add the title "The Ten Essentials".

5. Click to add the text "Extra clothing".

6. Press Enter and continue typing the remaining bulleted items as shown below:

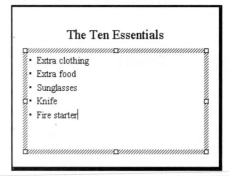

Saving a Presentation

1. Choose File>Save As.

2. Navigate to your **Work in Progress** folder from the Save in drop-down list box.

3. Name the file "Project A - Backcountry Almanac".

4. Click Save and leave this file open for the following exercises.

Once a presentation has been saved and named, you can do a quick save at any time by pressing Control-S.

To insert a new slide, use the Control-M shortcut.

Changing the Slide Layout

1. Click on the Common Tasks drop-down list box.

2. Choose Slide Layout.

3. Click on the 2 Column Text AutoLayout (third option, first row).

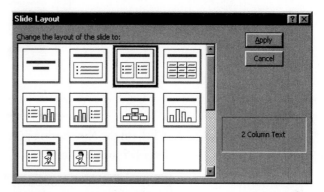

4. Choose Apply.

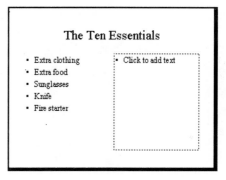

5. Click to add the text shown below.

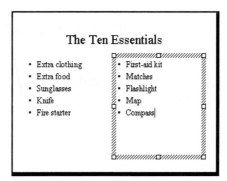

6. Press Control-S to save your presentation.

Changing Bullets to AutoNumbers

1. Select the first five bulleted items in the left placeholder.

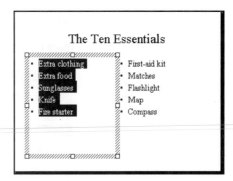

2. Click on the Numbering button on the Formatting toolbar to apply the numbers 1-5 to these items.

The Bullet and Numbering buttons on the Formatting toolbar are toggle buttons. If you press them once, the formatting is applied. If you press these buttons a second time, the formatting is removed or turned off.

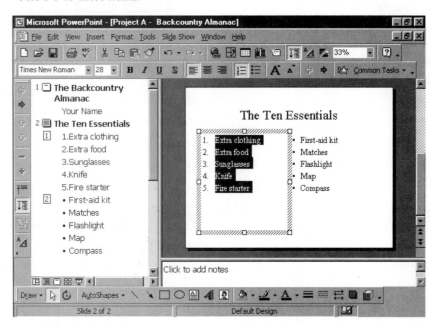

3. Select the five bulleted items in the right placeholder.

4. Choose Format>Bullets and Numbering.

5. Click on the Numbered tab.

6. Choose the first numbering format to apply Arabic numerals and click the Start at spin box to set the number to 6.

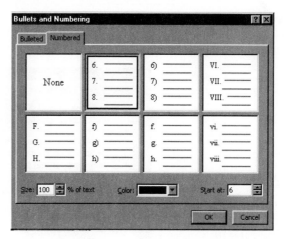

When you change the slide layout, the existing text will automatically adjust.

7. Click OK.

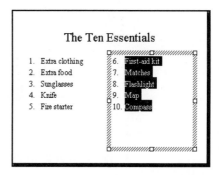

8. Use the Bulleted List AutoLayout to add the following slides:

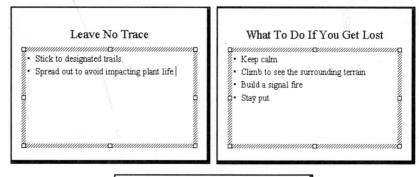

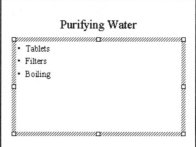

9. Press Control-S to Save your presentation.

Switching Views

1. Click on the Outline View button on the Views toolbar to switch to Outline view.

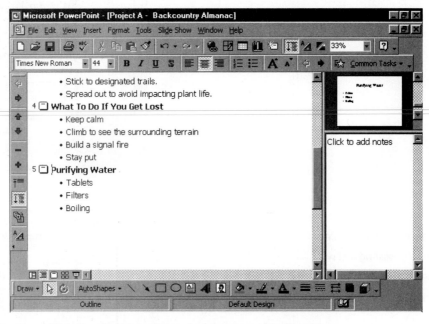

In addition to changing views from the toolbar at the bottom of the screen, you can also click on View on the Menu bar to select the appropriate view.

2. Go to Slide 3 and click at the end of the second bulleted item.

3. Press Enter to insert a new bullet.

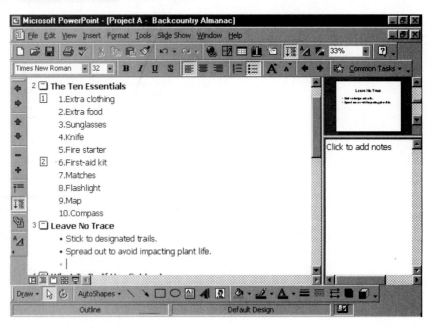

In Outline view, press the Tab key to demote an item. Press Shift-Tab to promote an item.

4. Type "Avoid soap or use biodegradable soap."

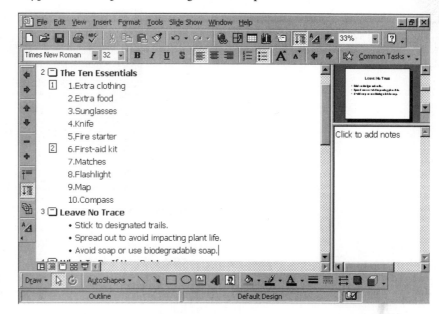

5. Click the Slide view button on the Views toolbar to switch to Slide view.

6. Save your presentation.

Applying a Design Template

1. Click on the Common Tasks drop-down list box.

2. Choose Apply Design Template.

3. Click on the Expedition Design Template.

At any time you can run a slide show from any view by pressing F5.

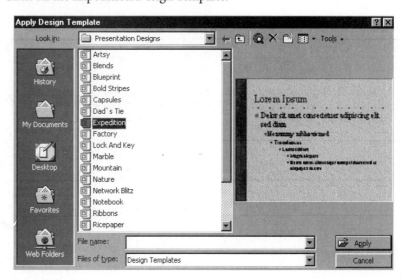

4. Choose Apply.

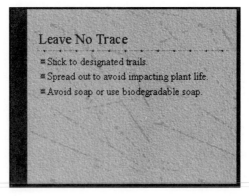

5. Save your presentation.

Previewing a Slide Show

1. Go to Slide 1.

2. Choose View>Slide Show.

To return to a previous slide press the Left Arrow key or right-click on the slide and choose Previous from the shortcut menu.

3. Click the left mouse button or press the Right Arrow key to advance from one slide to the next until you have viewed the entire presentation.

4. At the black screen, click to exit.

5. Save your presentation.

6. Exit PowerPoint.

Project B: Fitness Facts

Use the AutoContent Wizard to Create a Presentation

1. Start the PowerPoint application.

2. Choose AutoContent Wizard and click OK.

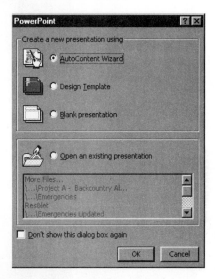

3. Click Next to advance to Step 2, Presentation Type.

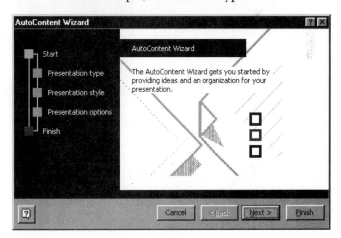

If the Office Assistant appears on your screen asking you if you want help, click No, don't provide help now.

4. Click on the Sales/Marketing category.

5. Click on Selling a Product or Service.

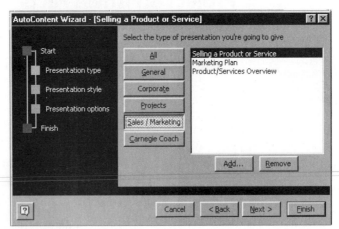

6. Click on Next to go to Step 3, Presentation Style.

7. Set the Presentation Style to On-screen presentation and click Next.

8. Type "Fitness Facts" in the Presentation title text box.

9. Type "easy ways to stay healthy..." in the Footers text box.

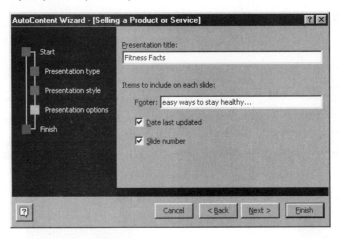

10. Click on Next and then click Finish.

11. Choose File>Save As.

12. Navigate to your **Work in Progress** folder. Save and name the file "Project B - Fitness Facts".

13. Choose Save and keep this file open for the following exercises.

The AutoContentWizard provides sample text and suggestions for preparing different types of presentations.

Adding Text to a Presentation

1. Select the text under the title in the Outline on the left of the screen and type your name.

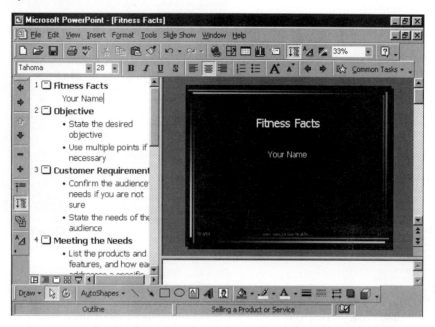

2. Select the two bulleted items under Slide 2, Objective in the Outline on the left of the screen.

3. Type "Learn about some easy ways to stay healthy."

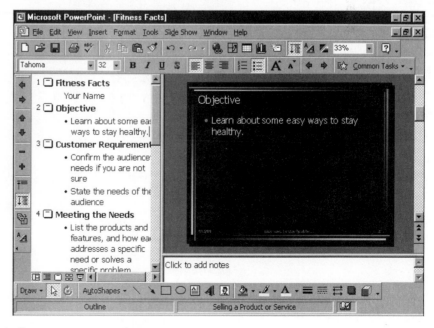

4. Save your presentation.

Deleting Slides

1. Click on the slide icon of Slide 4 in the Outline to select all of the text.

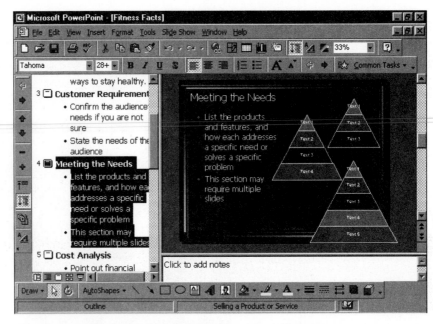

2. Scroll down the Outline until Slide 7 appears on the screen.

3. Hold down the Shift key and click on the Slide icon of Slide 7 to select Slides 4-7.

If the sample text inserted by the AutoContent Wizard doesn't apply to your presentation, you can simply select it and press the Delete key to remove it.

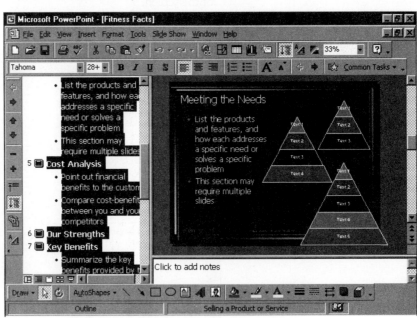

4. Press the Delete key and choose OK to delete Slides 4-7.

5. Save your presentation.

Adding Text to a Presentation

1. Go to Slide 3.

2. Select the title, "Customer Requirements," and type "Three Keys to Fitness".

3. Replace the bulleted items with the text shown.

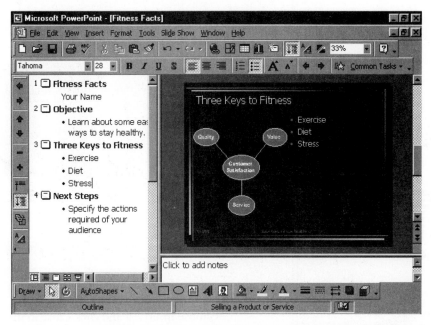

If you want to insert text on top of an object, use a text box.

4. Replace the text in the text boxes of the diagram as shown. The text box in the middle will read "Keys to Fitness." Type "Exercise" in the upper left text box; type "Diet" in the upper right text box; and type "Stress" in the bottom text box.

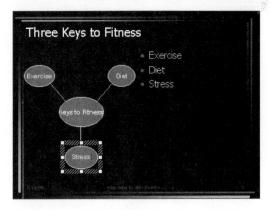

5. Save your presentation.

Copying Slides from a Presentation

1. Click after the last bulleted item on Slide 3.

2. Choose Insert>Slides from Files.

3. Click on the Browse button.

4. Navigate to the **SF-PowerPoint** folder and select the **Keys to Fitness** file. Select it and click Open.

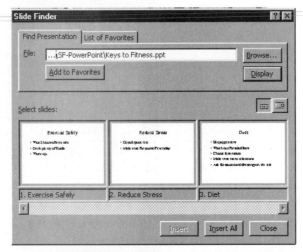

The total number of slides in the presentation will show in the Status bar at the bottom of the screen.

5. Choose Insert All and click Close to insert three new slides after Slide 3. There should now be a total of seven slides in this presentation.

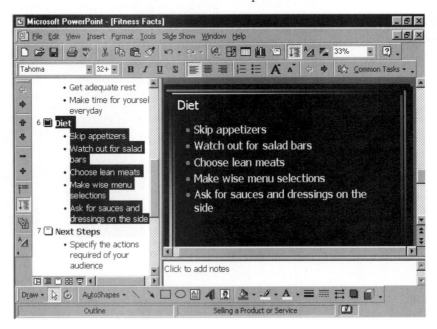

Control-H is the keyboard shortcut for Replace.

6. Switch to Slide view.

7. Go to Slide 7 and replace the existing text with the text shown.

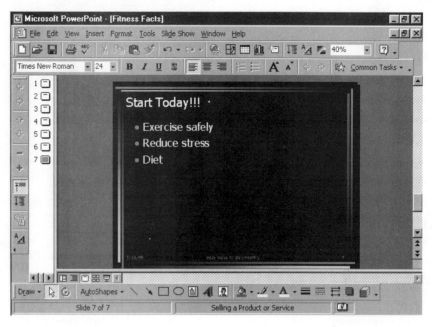

8. Save your presentation.

Find and Replace Text

1. Go to Slide 1.

2. Choose Edit>Replace.

3. Type "fluids" in the Find what text box.

4. Type "water" in the Replace with text box.

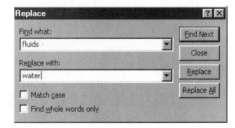

If you check the Match case checkbox in the Replace dialog box, PowerPoint will only find and replace the text exactly as it is typed.

By choosing Replace All at the Replace dialog box, PowerPoint searches and replaces all occurrences of the text throughout the entire presentation without stopping at each occurrence for validation before making the replacement. This is considered a global search and replace.

5. Choose Find Next.

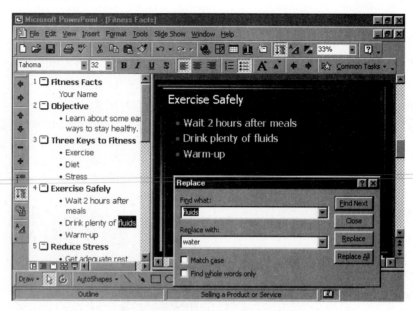

6. Choose Replace when PowerPoint selects the word "fluids."

7. Click OK at the prompt "PowerPoint has finished searching the presentation."

8. Close the Replace dialog box.

9. Save your presentation.

Insert Headers and Footers

1. Go to Slide 1.

2. If necessary, switch to Slide view.

3. Choose View>Header and Footer.

4. Click on the Fixed radio button and type "October 15, 2001".

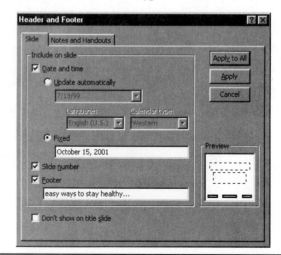

5. Choose Apply to All.

6. Switch to Slide Show view and preview your entire presentation to see the footers.

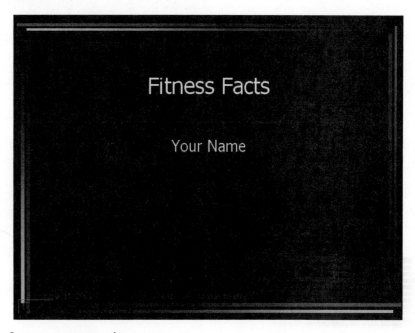

7. Save your presentation.

Modifying the Slide Master

1. Choose View>Master>Slide Master.

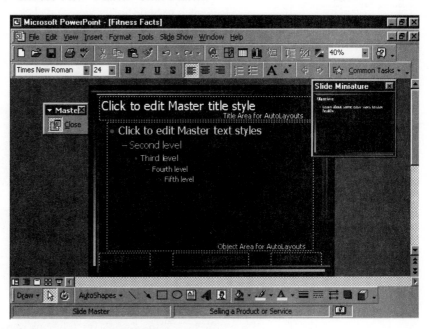

2. Select the text "Click to edit Master title style."

Footers are optional and may be more useful for audience handouts than they are during a slide show.

3. Change the font to Impact and the font size to 40.

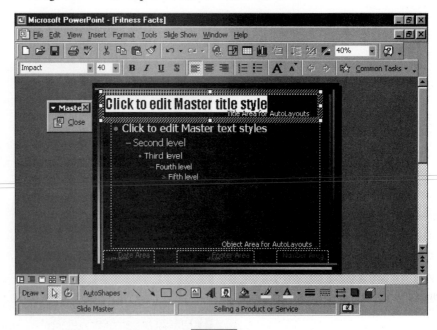

When you change the Slide Master, all of the slides in the presentation are modified at the same time.

4. Click Close on the Master Slide toolbar.

5. Preview each of the slides to see the impact of changing the Master Slide. Save your presentation.

Rearrange the Slides in Slide Sorter View

1. Switch to Slide Sorter view and click on Slide 6.

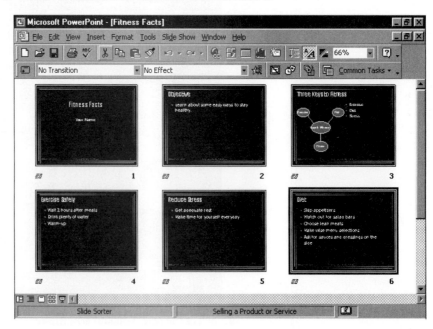

2. Drag Slide 6 to the left of Slide 5.

3. When a vertical line appears to the left of Slide 5, release the left mouse button.

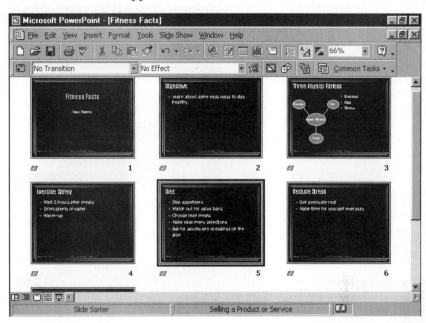

4. Save your presentation.

Rearranging Slides in Outline View

1. Switch to Outline view.

2. Click on the Slide 5 icon in the Outline to select all of the text in Slide 5.

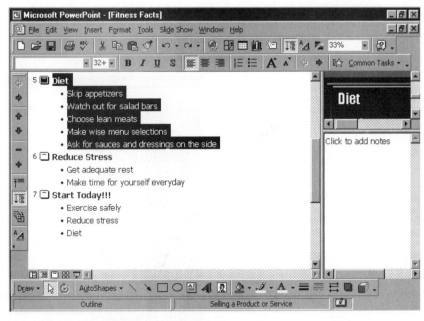

3. Drag the selected text down below the last bulleted item in Slide 6.

4. When a horizontal line appears below the last bulleted item in Slide 6, release the left mouse button.

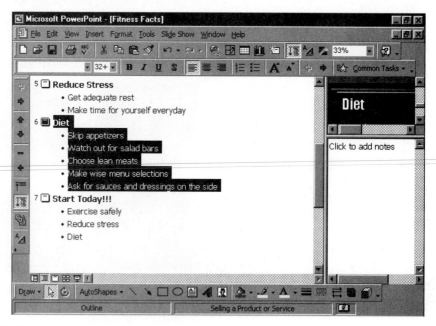

You can also click on the Move buttons to change the order of a slide in Outline or Normal view.

5. Save your presentation.

Apply a New Design Template

1. Switch to Slide view.

2. Go to Slide 1.

3. Click on the Common Tasks drop-down list box and choose Apply Design Template.

4. Click on Mountain.

You can also apply a design template by choosing Format>Apply Design Template.

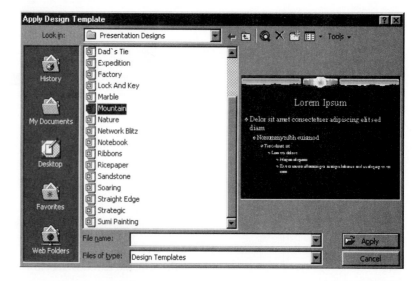

Applying a design template adjusts the position of text and objects on the slides. If you apply a new design template to your presentation, be certain to view the entire presentation to ensure that items on the slide are appropriately placed.

5. Choose Apply.

6. Save your presentation.

7. Close your presentation.

8. Exit PowerPoint.

Notes:

Project C: Mastering Golf

Entering Text in Different Views

1. Start PowerPoint.

2. Choose Blank presentation.

3. Click OK.

4. Choose the Title Slide AutoLayout and click OK.

5. Type "Mastering Golf" as the title and your own name as the subtitle.

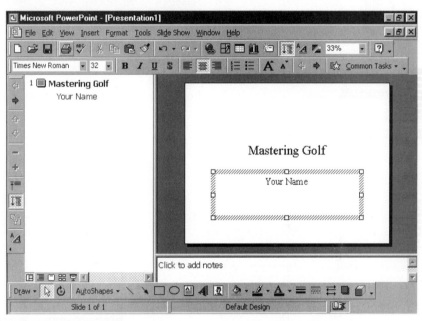

6. Click after Your Name in the Outline on the left and press Enter.

Promoting and Demoting Text

1. Click the Promote button ◄ on the Outlining toolbar.

2. Type "Compare Clubs" and press Enter.

3. Click the Demote button ► on the Outlining toolbar.

4. Type the bulleted items shown.

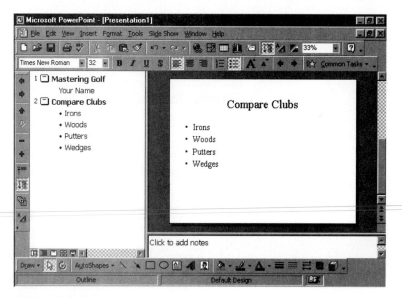

You can also use Tab and Shift Tab to demote and promote respectively.

5. Switch to Slide view.

6. Choose Insert>New Slide..

7. Choose the Bulleted List AutoLayout and click OK.

8. Type the text shown.

> ## Let The Club Do The Work
>
> - Make a full turn away from the ball
> - Sweep through the ball
> - Always follow through

9. Repeats steps 6-8 to create the following slides:

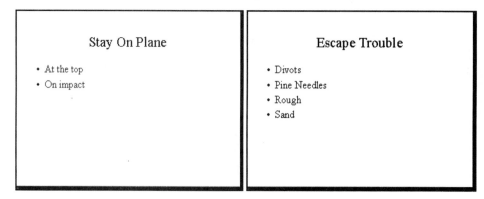

10. Choose File>Save As and name the presentation "Project C - Mastering Golf" into your **Work in Progress** folder. Click Save and keep the file open for the following exercises.

Apply a Design Template

1. Choose Format>Apply Design Template.

2. Choose Dad's Tie and click Apply.

3. Save your presentation.

Change the Line Spacing

1. Go to Slide 1.

2. Choose View>Master>Slide Master.

3. Select the bulleted items in the lower placeholder.

4. Choose Format>Line Spacing.

5. Set the Line spacing to 2 Lines and the Before paragraph spacing to 0.5 Lines. Click OK.

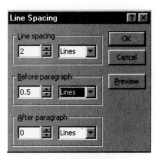

6. Click Close on the Master toolbar ![Master Close] to return to Slide view.

7. Scroll through the slides to see the change in line spacing on all slides.

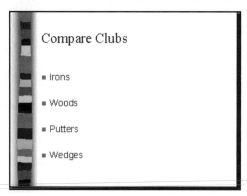

There are 72 points in a vertical inch.

8. Save your presentation.

Changing the Font

1. Go to Slide 2. Select the Compare Clubs title.

3. Choose Format>Font.

4. Change the Font to Comic, the Font style to Bold, the Size to 48, and the Color to turquoise (fifth color chip).

5. Click OK and click off of the selected text to view the changes you've made.

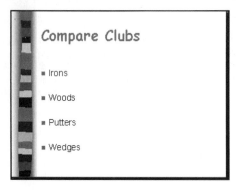

If you can't find the Comic, choose a different font. Comic is included with PowerPoint and may be found on your application CD-ROM.

6. Save your presentation.

Using the Format Painter

1. Go to Slide 2. Select the "Compare Clubs" title.

2. Double-click on the Format Painter button 🖌 on the Standard toolbar.

3. Go to Slide 3.

If you only click once on the Format Painter, it will only stay on for one selection. To apply formatting to several selections, be certain to double-click.

4. Drag the mouse, which has changed from a pointer shape to a paint brush, across the "Let The Club Do The Work" title.

5. Repeat steps 4 to apply the formatting to the titles in Slides 4 and 5.

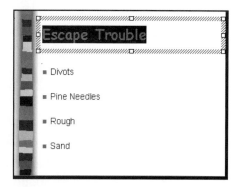

6. Click on the Format Painter button to turn the Format Painter off.

Changing the Alignment of Text

1. Go to Slide 2. Click anywhere in the title.

2. Choose Format>Alignment>Center.

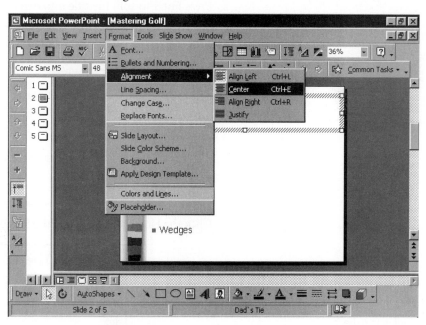

3. Go to Slide 3. Click anywhere in the title.

The keyboard shortcut to left align text is Control-L. To right align text, the shortcut is Control-R.

4. Press Control-E to center the text.

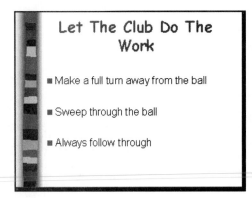

5. Go to Slides 4 and 5 and center the title text using either of the alignment methods mentioned above.

6. Press Control-S to Save your presentation.

Using Undo and Redo

1. Go to Slide 3. Click after the word "Club" in the title.

2. Press Enter to split the title into two separate lines.

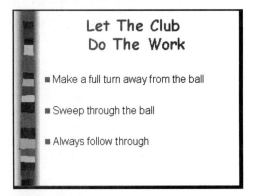

3. Click the Undo button  on the Standard toolbar.

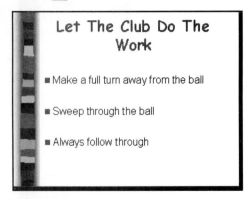

You can also access Undo and Redo from Edit on the Menu bar or use the keyboard shortcuts, Control-Z and Control-Y.

4. Click the Redo button ⌐ on the Standard toolbar. Save your presentation.

Cut and Paste Text

1. Switch to Outline view.

2. Go to Slide 5.

3. Select the last bulleted item, "Sand."

The keyboard shortcut for Cut is Control-X or you can also click on the Cut button on the Standard toolbar.

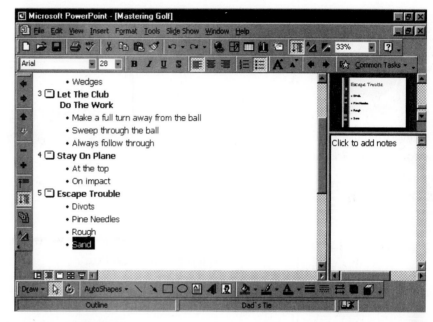

4. Choose Edit>Cut.

5. Click before the "D" in "Divots."

6. Choose Edit>Paste. Save your presentation.

Control-V is the keyboard shortcut for Paste. Control-P is reserved for Print. You can also click on the Paste button on the Standard toolbar.

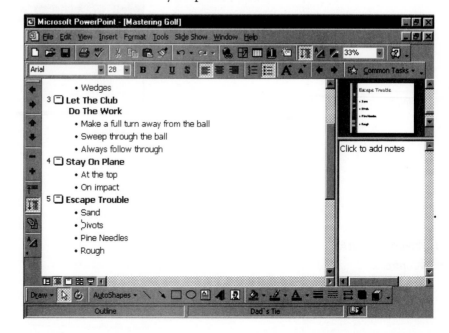

Creating Text Boxes

1. Switch to Slide view.

2. Go to Slide 1.

3. Click on AutoShapes on the Drawing toolbar.

4. Point to Stars and Banners and choose Explosion 2 (second option, first row).

5. Drag to draw a shape in the lower-right corner of the slide as shown.

If you make a mistake when drawing the shape, click the Undo button or choose Edit>Undo.

6. Choose Insert>Text Box.

7. Position the mouse, which now appears as a crosshair, on top of the shape and drag to draw a text box.

8. Type "Tip" in the text box.

9. Press Control-E to center "Tip."

10. Save your presentation.

The keyboard shortcut for Undo is Control-Z.

Copy and Paste

1. Click on the Text Box you created in the previous exercise.

2. Hold down the Shift key and click on the shape so that both the text box and the shape are selected as shown.

3. Choose Edit>Copy.

4. Go to Slide 2.

5. Choose Edit>Paste.

6. Go to each of the other slides in this presentation and Paste the shape and text box on these remaining slides.

7. Save your presentation.

Control-C is the keyboard shortcut for Copy. You can also click the Copy button on the Standard toolbar.

Using Word Art

1. Go to Slide 1.

2. Click anywhere in the Title placeholder to make it active.

3. Click on the border of the Title placeholder to select it. A dotted border around the placeholder indicates that the placeholder is selected.

As you are pasting objects to slides, if you see a light bulb appear, you can click on it to get a tip informing you that an easier way to copy something to all slides is to modify the Slide Master. Click OK to close the tip.

4. Press the Delete key to delete the title placeholder.

5. Choose Insert>Picture>Word Art.

6. Choose the WordArt style in the fourth row, fourth option of the WordArt Gallery dialog box.

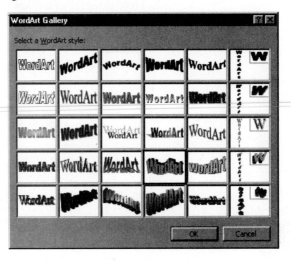

You can also access WordArt by clicking on the WordArt button on the Drawing toolbar.

7. Click OK.

8. Type "Mastering Golf".

9. Set the Font to Comic, the Size to 96, and click the Bold button.

10. Click OK.

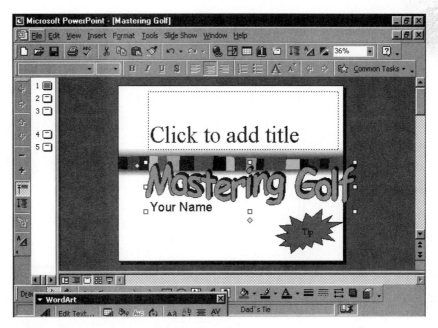

*Remember that a place-
holder is activated if the
border appears with
diagonal lines. To select a
placeholder, such as when
you wish to delete it, you
must click on the border a
second time. The place-
holder is selected when it
appears with a dotted
border.*

11. Click in the "Click to add title" placeholder.

12. Click on the border of the "Click to add title" placeholder.

13. Press the Delete key.

14. Click on the "Mastering Golf" WordArt object.

15. Position the mouse pointer on top of the WordArt object.

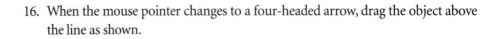

If the title placeholder does not appear in your slide, skip steps 11-13.

16. When the mouse pointer changes to a four-headed arrow, drag the object above the line as shown.

17. Save your presentation.

Check Spelling

The keyboard shortcut for Spellcheck is F7. You can also click on the Spelling button on the Standard toolbar.

1. Choose Tools>Spelling.

2. Correct any errors.

3. Save your presentation.

4. Go to Slide 1.

5. Switch to Slide Show view and preview the entire presentation.

6. Close the **Mastering Golf** file.

7. Exit PowerPoint.

Project D: Easy & Elegant Baking

Open an Existing Presentation

1. Start the PowerPoint application.

2. Select Open an existing presentation and click OK.

3. Navigate to the **SF-PowerPoint folder**, click on the **Baking** file, and choose Open.

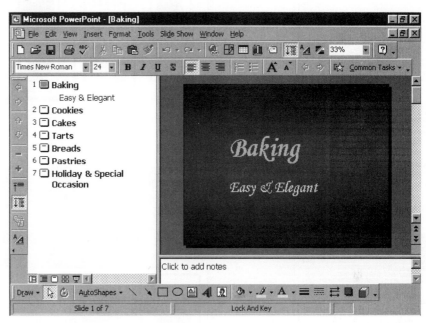

If PowerPoint is already open, choose File>Open to access an existing PowerPoint presentation.

4. Choose File>Save As and name the file "Project E - Baking Updated". Save it into your **Work in Progress** folder.

5. Click Save and keep the file open for the following exercises.

Insert ClipArt

1. Switch to Slide view.

2. Go to Slide 1.

3. Choose Insert>Picture>ClipArt.

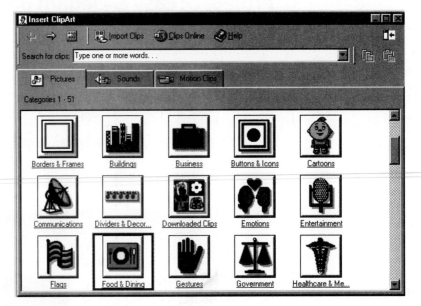

4. Click on Food & Dining.

5. Click on the ClipArt image of the bread basket.

If you can't find the ClipArt image of the bread basket, use a different ClipArt image.

6. Click on Insert clip from the top of the list of callout options.

7. Close the Insert ClipArt dialog box.

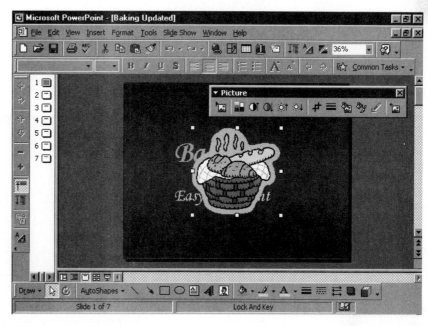

8. Save the presentation.

Resizing Objects

1. Go to Slide 1.

2. If necessary, click on the ClipArt image to select it.

3. Position your mouse pointer on the lower-left corner handle of the image.

4. When the mouse pointer changes to a double-headed arrow, drag up and to the right to resize the image as shown.

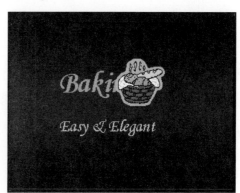

When an object is selected, sizing handles or selection handles will appear around all sides of the object.

5. Save your presentation.

Moving Objects

1. Position the mouse pointer on the ClipArt image.

2. When the mouse pointer changes to a four-headed arrow, drag up and to the right to move the object as shown.

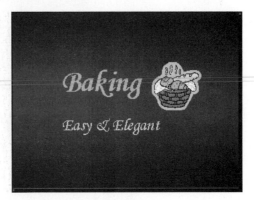

Creating Images with the Drawing Toolbar

1. Go to Slide 1.

2. Click on AutoShapes on the Drawing toolbar.

3. Point to Basic Shapes and choose the Heart shape (sixth row, first option).

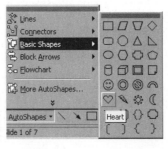

When the mouse pointer changes to a double-headed arrow, you can resize an object. When the mouse pointer changes to a four-headed arrow you can move an object.

4. Drag in the lower-left corner of Slide 1 to draw a heart like the one shown.

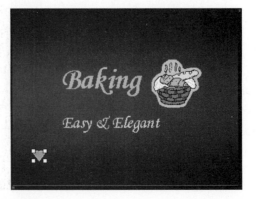

5. Save your presentation.

Copy Objects

1. With the heart still selected, hold down the Control key on your keyboard and drag to the right.

2. Release the left mouse button and the Control key and choose Copy Here.

You can also copy objects using Copy and Paste. If you choose this option, you'll have to move the copied objects.

3. Repeats steps 1 and 2 to create a line of hearts as shown.

Aligning Objects

1. Click on the first heart to select it.

2. Hold down the Shift key and click on all of the remaining hearts to select them.

3. Click on Draw on the Drawing toolbar.

4. Point to Align or Distribute and choose Align Top.

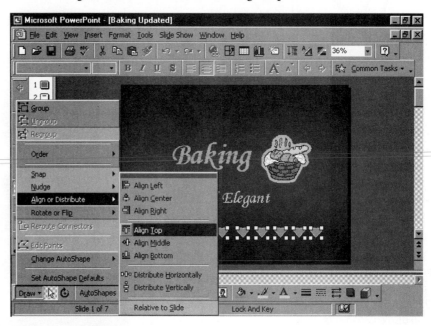

5. Save your presentation.

Grouping Objects

1. With the hearts still selected, click Draw on the Drawing toolbar.

2. Click on Group to make all of the hearts one object.

3. Save your presentation.

Rotating Objects

1. Go to Slide 1.

2. Click on the ClipArt image of the bread basket.

3. Click on the Free Rotate button on the Drawing toolbar.

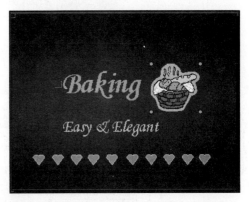

4. Position the mouse, which now appears as a Free Rotate object, on the lower-left free rotate handle.

5. Drag up and to the right to slightly rotate the object as shown.

6. Click on the Free Rotate button to toggle it off.

7. Save your presentation.

Insert Photographs from File

1. Go to Slide 2.

2. Choose Insert>Picture>From File.

3. At the Insert Picture dialog box, navigate to the **SF-PowerPoint** folder and select the **Cookie** file.

If you deselected the hearts, hold down the Shift key and click on each heart again.

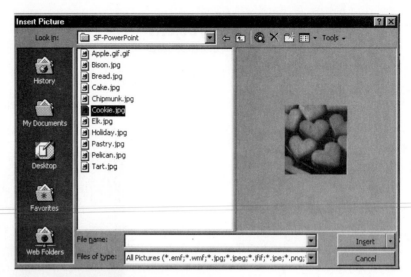

4. Click on the Cookie file and choose Insert.

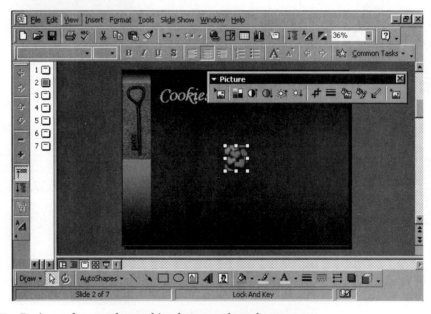

5. Resize and move the cookie photograph as shown.

6. With the photograph of the cookie still selected, choose Format>Picture.

Close or move the Picture toolbar if it is in the way.

7. Click on the Colors and Lines tab.

8. Set the Line Color to Black and the Line Weight to 4 pt.

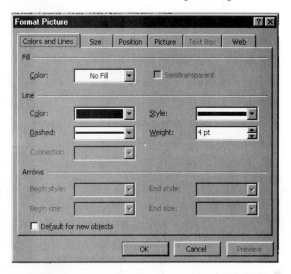

9. Click OK.

From the Format Picture dialog box, you can change the size of the object, its position, border, and fill.

10. Save your presentation.

11. Repeat steps 2-10 to create the slides shown in the following images.

If you accidentally double-click on the ClipArt image, the Format Object dialog box will be displayed. If this happens, close the Format dialog box and continue working.

12. Save your presentation.

Filling Objects

1. Go to Slide 1.

2. Click on the Hearts object at the bottom of the screen.

3. Choose Format>Object.

4. Click on the Color and Lines tab.

5. Click on the Color drop-down list box under Fill and choose Fill Effects.

6. Click on the Texture tab.

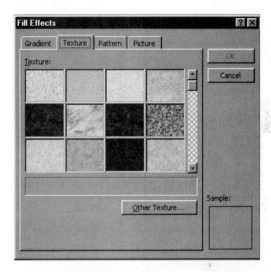

7. Click on the Stationery fill effect (fourth option, first row) and choose OK.

8. Click OK again to fill the object with the texture.

9. Save your presentation.

10. Switch to Slide Show view and preview your presentation.

11. Close the Baking Updated file.

12. Exit PowerPoint.

In addition to filling an object with a texture, you can also fill an object with a gradient, pattern, or selected picture.

Notes:

Project E: Wildflower Spas

Create a New Presentation from Existing Slides

1. Start the PowerPoint application.

2. Choose Open an existing presentation.

3. Navigate to the **SF-PowerPoint** folder and open the **Wildflower Spas** file.

4. Click to add subtitle and type "Your Name".

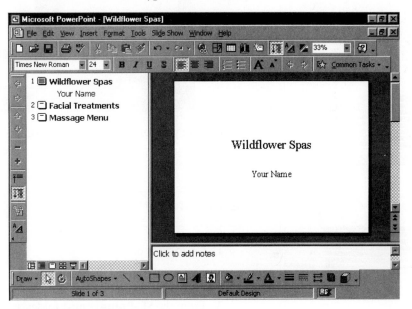

5. Go to Slide 3.

6. Choose Insert>Slides from Files.

7. Click Browse at the Slide Finder dialog box.

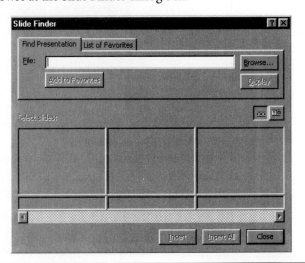

8. From the **SF-PowerPoint** folder, select the **Spa Therapies** and click Insert All.

9. Click Close.

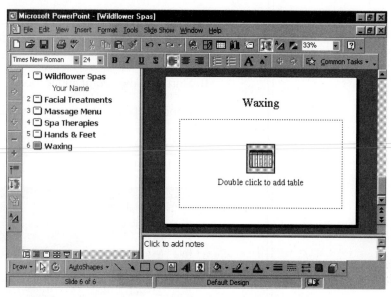

10. Save your presentation as "Project E - Wildflower Spas" into your **Work in Progress** folder. Keep the presentation file open for the following exercises.

Import Text from Word

1. Go to Slide 6.

2. Choose Insert Slides from Outline.

3. From the **SF-PowerPoint** folder, select the **Wildflower Spa Packages** file.

4. Choose Insert.

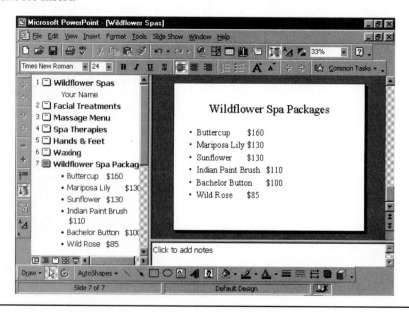

Add Tables

When you click on one of the AutoLayouts at the left, the name of the AutoLayout appears in the lower-right corner of the dialog box.

1. Go to Slide 2.

2. Choose Format>Slide Layout.

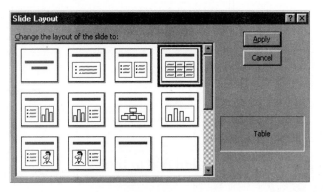

3. Click the Table AutoLayout and choose Apply.

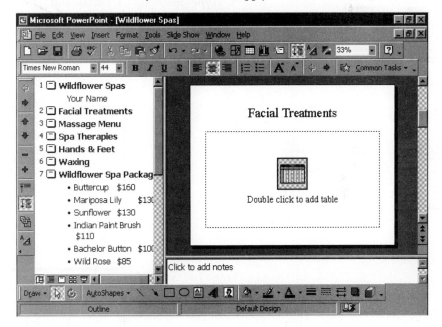

4. Double click to add table.

5. Set the Number of columns to 2 and the Number of rows to 6 at the Insert Table dialog box.

A spin box allows you to incrementally increase or decrease an amount by clicking on the up or down arrows.

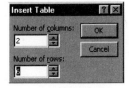

6. Click OK.

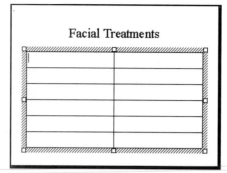

7. Save your presentation.

Add Text to Tables

1. Type "Rejuvenating Facial" and press Tab.

2. Type "$85" and press Tab.

3. In the other cells of the table, type the following text.

Facial Treatments

Rejuvenating Facial	$85
Deep Cleansing Facial	$70
Glycolic Acid Treatment	$45
Firming Treatment	$25
Biological Peel	$45
Mini Facial	$35

4. Add the tables shown to Slides 3, 4, 5, and 6.

Massage Menu

Half-hour Massage	$30
One hour Massage	$55
Hour & ½ Massage	$75

Spa Therapies

European Herbal Wrap	$35
Body Buff	$50
Moor Mud Body Mask	$70
Salt Glow	$35
Steam Treatment	$10

Hands & Feet

Paraffin Wax	$15
Polish	$10
Manicure	$35
Pedicure	$35
Manicure & Pedicure	$55

Waxing

Full Leg	$65
Lower Leg	$35
Upper Leg	$35
Bikini	$25
Chin	$12
Brow	$15

To go to any cell of a table, you can either click in the cell or press Tab to move to the next cell. Press Shift-Tab to move to the previous cell.

5. Save your presentation.

Adding and Removing Table Rows

1. Go to Slide 4.

2. Switch to Slide view.

3. Choose View>Toolbars>Tables and Borders.

4. Click anywhere in the Body Buff row of the table.

5. Choose Table>Insert Rows Below from the Tables and Borders toolbar.

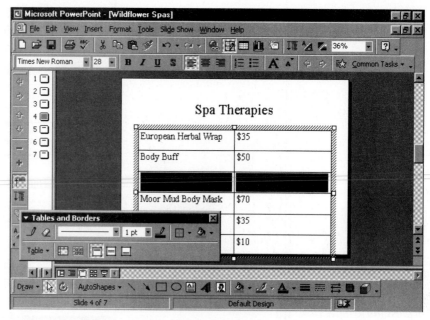

6. Type "Seaweed Body Mask", press Tab, and type "$65".

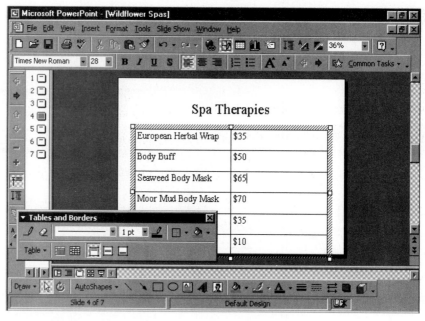

If necessary, move the Tables and Borders toolbar by dragging the blue title bar.

7. Go to Slide 5.

8. If necessary, choose View>Toolbars>Tables and Borders to make the Tables and Borders toolbar appear on the screen.

9. Click anywhere in the last row of the table.

10. Choose Table>Select Row from the Tables and Borders toolbar.

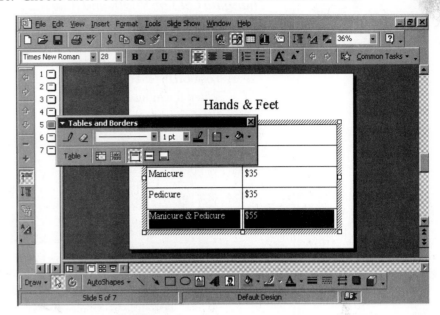

11. Choose Table>Delete Row.

12. Go to Slide 6.

13. Click anywhere in the Brow row.

14. Choose Table>Insert Rows Above.

15. Type "Upper Lip". Press Tab.

16. Type "$13".

You can apply formatting such as bold, italics, font face, font size, and color to table text just as you do to any text. Simply select the text within the table and choose the appropriate formatting command or button.

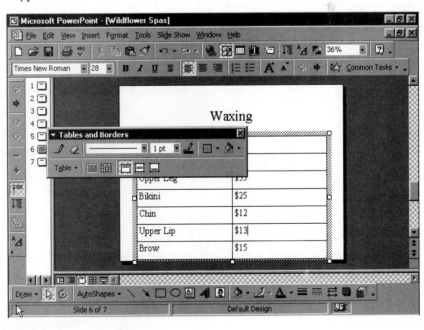

17. Save your presentation.

Changing Column Width and Row Height

1. Go to Slide 2.

2. Position the mouse pointer on the line that separates Column A and Column B. When the mouse changes to a double-headed arrow, drag to the right to resize the columns as shown.

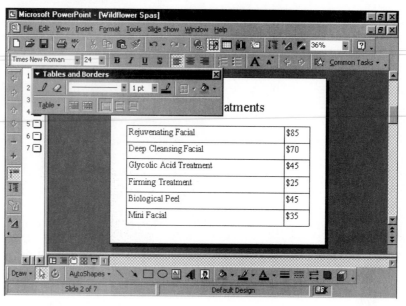

4. Repeat steps 1-3 to resize the columns in slides 3, 4, 5, and 6.

5. Go to Slide 3.

6. Position the mouse pointer on the horizontal line that separates Row 1 from Row 2. When the shape of the mouse pointer changes to a double-headed arrow, drag up to resize the row height as shown.

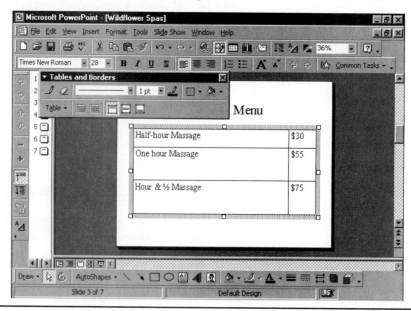

The shape of the mouse indicates its function. For example, a double-headed arrow generally indicates that you can resize an object while a four-headed arrow indicates that you can move the object.

If the Select Table option is dimmed or grayed out, the table may already be selected. A table is selected when the border appears as a series of dots. If the table is not selected, click anywhere within the table to activate it, then choose Table>Select Table.

7. Resize the row height of the remaining rows in the table.

8. Click on the table border. When the shape of the mouse changes to a four-headed arrow, drag the table down to center it on the slide.

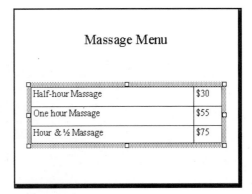

9. Save your presentation.

Aligning Text Within a Table

1. Go to Slide 2.

2. If necessary, choose View>Toolbars>Tables and Borders.

3. Choose Table>Select Table.

4. Click on the Center Vertically button [≡] on the Tables and Borders toolbar to vertically center the text within the cells as shown.

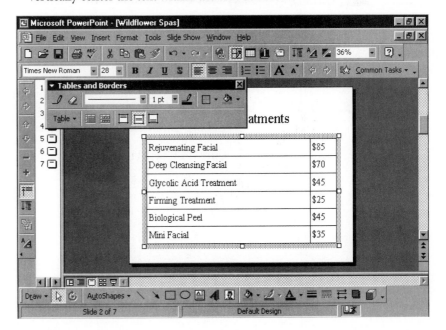

5. Repeat steps 2-5 to vertically center the text within the tables on slides 3-6.

6. Go to Slide 2.

7. Click anywhere in Column B.

8. Choose Table>Select Column from the Tables and Borders toolbar.

9. Press Control-R to align all of the text in Column B to the right of the cell as shown.

To right-align the text in Column B, you can also click on the Right Align button on the Formatting toolbar.

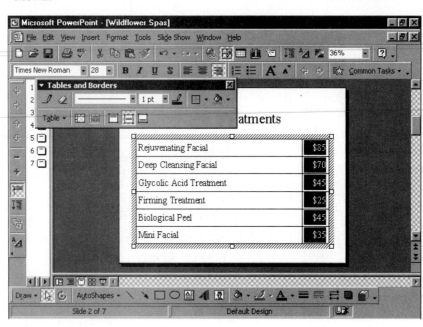

10. Repeat step 9 to right-align the text in Column B on Slides 3-6.

11. Close the Tables and Borders toolbar.

12. Save your presentation.

Applying a Design Template

1. Choose Common Tasks>Apply Design Template.

2. Click on Blueprint and choose Apply.

3. Save your presentation.

Adding Borders and Shading to a Table

1. Go to Slide 2.

2. If the Tables and Borders toolbar is not visible, choose View>Toolbars>Tables and Borders.

3. Click anywhere within the table on Slide 2.

4. Change the Border Width to 6 pt.

5. Click on the Draw Table button ✐ to activate it.

6. Drag across the top and bottom borders of the table to create the thicker border shown.

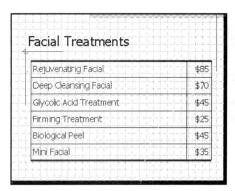

7. Click anywhere in Column B.

8. Choose Table>Select Column.

9. Click on the drop-down list box next to Fill Color ▵ ▾.

10. Choose Fill Effects and click on the Texture tab.

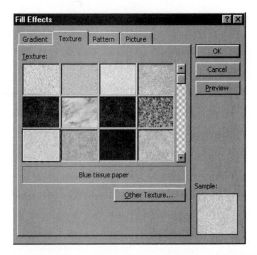

If you make a mistake when drawing the borders, you can click on the Undo button or use the keyboard shortcut, Control-Z, and try again.

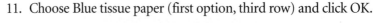

In addition to applying textures to table cells, you can also apply gradients, patterns, and pictures. Fill Effects add emphasis both on-screen and in print.

11. Choose Blue tissue paper (first option, third row) and click OK.

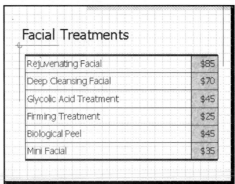

12. Repeat steps 2-11 to change the top and bottom borders and add the same fill effect to Column B on Slides 3-6.

13. Save your presentation.

Adding AutoNumber Bullets

1. Go to Slide 7.

2. If necessary, close the Tables and Borders toolbar.

3. Click after Buttercup and press Tab three times.

4. Click after Mariposa Lily and press Tab three times.

5. Repeat step 3 or 4 on each of the remaining lines and press Tab as needed to align the text.

6. Select the six bulleted items.

7. Choose Format>Bullets and Numbering.

8. Click on the Numbered tab and choose the option immediately to the right of None.

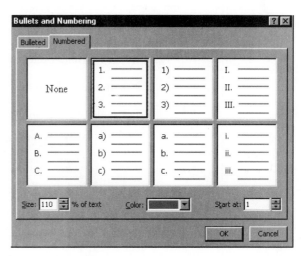

9. Click OK.

10. If necessary, delete any extra tabs to align the text as shown.

11. Save your presentation.

You can further customize numbers by changing the size, color, and starting number.

To delete extra tabs, click before the dollar amount and press backspace or click after the name of the spa package and press delete.

Customizing Bullets

1. Select the six numbered items on Slide 7.

2. Choose Format>Bullets and Numbering.

3. Click on the Bulleted tab.

4. Choose the second option in the second row.

In addition to customizing bullets by choosing different symbols, you can further customize bullets by changing the color and the size of the bullet.

5. Click OK.

8. Save your presentation.

Wrapping Text in a Text Box

1. Go to Slide 1.

2. Choose Insert>Text Box.

3. Position the mouse in the upper-right corner of the slide and drag to draw a text box as shown.

If the text in the text box does not appear centered, make certain that the text box is selected before pressing Control-E. You can also click on the Center button on the Formatting toolbar to center the text.

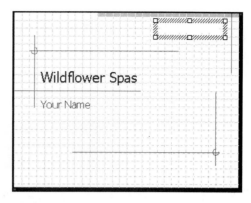

4. Type "Treat Yourself to a Luxurious Day at the Spa" and allow the text to wrap to the next line as shown.

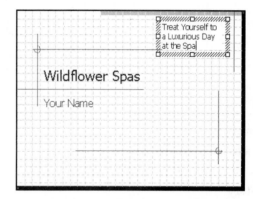

5. Press Control-E to center the text in the text box.

6. If necessary, move the text box to position it as shown.

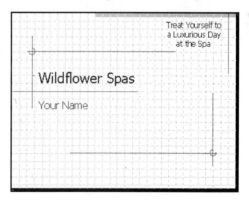

7. Save your presentation.

You can move a text box just as you move any object. Select the object. Position the mouse on the border. When the shape of the mouse changes to a four-headed arrow, drag the object to move it.

Adding Slide Transitions

1. Switch to Slide Sorter view.

2. Choose Edit>Select All.

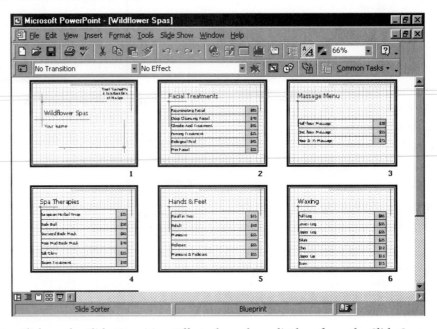

You can select none, one, or all slides. You can also select designated slides by holding down the Shift key and clicking on the slides to be selected.

3. Click on the Slide Transition Effects drop-down list box from the Slide Sorter toolbar.

6. Choose Dissolve.

7. Click on the Slide icon in the lower-left corner of any slide to preview the dissolve transition.

8. Save your presentation.

Applying Animation

1. If necessary, scroll down so that Slide 7 is visible on your screen.

2. Click on the white background to the right of Slide 7 to deselect the slides.

3. Click on Slide 7 so that only Slide 7 is selected.

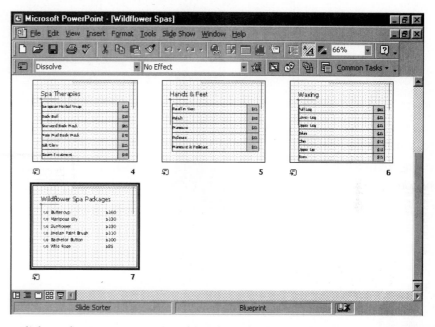

4. Click on the Preset Animation drop-down list box on the Slide Sorter toolbar.

5. Choose Dissolve.

6. Click on the second icon in the lower-left corner of Slide 7 to see a preview of the animation.

7. Save your presentation.

Adding Speaker's Notes

1. Go to Slide 7 of your presentation.

2. Choose View>Notes Page.

3. Zoom to 66%.

You can zoom to any percentage by typing a number in the Zoom Text box and pressing Enter.

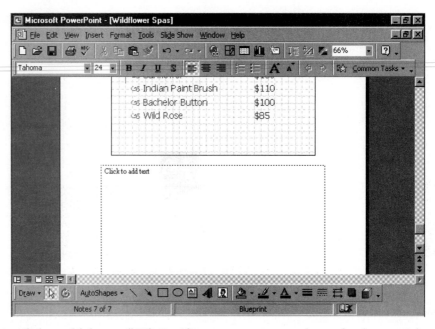

4. Click to add the text "Gift Certificates - an unexpected treat for that special someone".

5. Save your presentation.

6. Go to Slide 1.

7. Switch to Slide Show view and preview your entire presentation.

8. Close your presentation and exit PowerPoint.

The keyboard shortcut F5 can be used to switch to Slide Show view at any time and from any view.

Project F: Washington Apples Online

Saving a PowerPoint Presentation as a Web Page

1. Start PowerPoint and choose Open an existing presentation.

2. From the **SF-PowerPoint** folder, open **Washington Apples Online**.

3. Choose File>Save as Web Page.

4. Save the file as "Project F - Washington Apples Online" into your **Work in Progress** folder. Be certain that the Save as type option is set to Web Page.

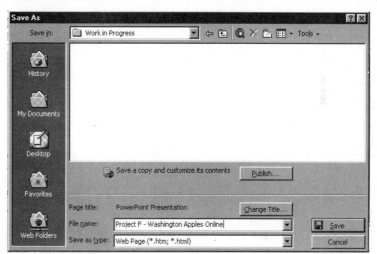

5. Keep the presentation file open for the following exercises.

Adding a New Slide

1. Switch to Slide view and go to Slide 1.

2. Choose New Slide from the Common Tasks drop-down list box.

3. Click on the Bulleted List AutoLayout.

The shortcut to insert a new slide is Control-M.

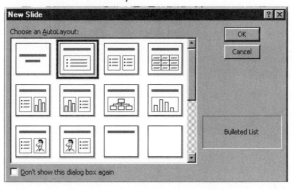

4. Click OK.

5. Type the following text:

```
Apples are:

• No fat
• #1 Fruit choice
• Source of fiber
• Cholesterol free
• Nature's health food
• Suitable to every taste
• Excellent substitute snack
```

6. Save your presentation.

Applying a Design Template

1. Click on the Common Tasks drop-down list box and choose Apply Design Template.

2. Click on Ribbons.

3. Choose Apply.

```
Apples are:

• No fat
• #1 Fruit choice
• Source of fiber
• Cholesterol free
• Nature's health food
• Suitable to every taste
• Excellent substitute snack
```

4. Save your presentation.

5. Close the PowerPoint application.

To apply a design template, you can also choose Format>Apply Design Template from the Menu bar.

View a PowerPoint Presentation in a Web Browser

1. Start your Web browser.

2. Choose File>Open if you are using Internet Explorer or File>Open Page if you are using Netscape.

3. Click Browse or Open File.

4. Navigate to your **Work in Progress** folder and select the **Project F - Washington Apples Online** file.

5. Choose OK or Open until the PowerPoint presentation appears in your browser as shown.

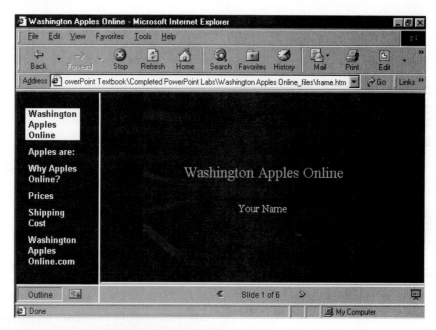

6. Click on each of the heading options at the left and notice how the contents in the frame on the right side of the screen changes.

7. Click back on **Washington Apples Online**, Slide 1 to return to the Home page of this Web site.

8. Leave the file open.

Viewing the HTML Source Code

1. Choose View>Source or View>Page Source from the Menu bar.

2. If necessary, maximize the screen containing the HTML source code.

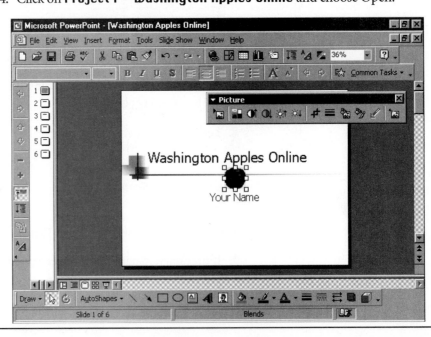

```
frame - Notepad
File  Edit  Search  Help
<html>

<head>
<meta http-equiv=Content-Type content="text/html; charset=windows-1252">
<meta name=ProgId content=PowerPoint.Slide>
<meta name=Generator content="Microsoft PowerPoint 9">
<link id=Main-File rel=Main-File href="../Washington%20Apples%20Online.htm">
<link rel=Preview href=preview.wmf>
<title>Washington Apples Online</title>
<![if !ppt]><script src=script.js></script><script>
<!--
var gNavLoaded = gOtlNavLoaded = gOtlLoaded = false;
function Load()
{
        str=document.location.hash,idx=str.indexOf('#')
        if(idx>=0) str=str.substr(1);
        if(str) PPTSld.location.replace(str);
}
//-->
</script><![endif]>
</head>

<frameset rows="*,25" frameborder=0>
 <frameset cols="20%,80%" id=PPTHorizAdjust framespacing=2>
  <frame src=outline.htm name=PPTOtl>
  <frameset rows="100%,*" id=PPTVertAdjust framespacing=2 frameborder=1
```

3. Close the HTML source code.

4. Close your Web browser.

Change the Design Template and Color Scheme

1. Start the PowerPoint application.

2. Choose File>Open.

3. Click on the drop-down list box next to Files of type and choose Web Pages.

4. Click on **Project F – Washington Apples Online** and choose Open.

5. Choose Format>Apply Design Template.

6. Choose the Blends presentation design and click Apply.

7. Choose Format>Slide Color Scheme.

8. If necessary, click on the Standard tab.

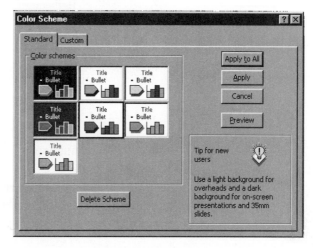

9. Click the third option in the second row.

10. Choose Apply to All.

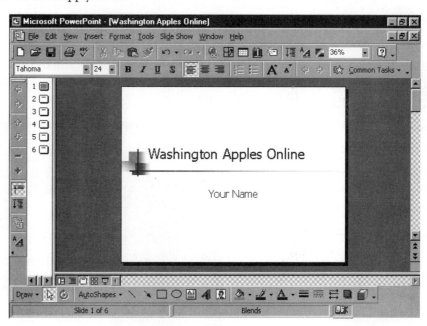

11. Go to Slide 4.

12. Click on the table and resize Column B as shown.

13. Save your presentation.

Creating Objects to be Used as Hyperlinks.

1. Go to Slide 1.

2. Choose Insert>Picture>From File.

3. Navigate to the **SF-PowerPoint** folder and click on **Apple.GIF** and choose Insert.

If you do not see the .GIF extension after apple, this just means that the extensions are not set to display on your computer. Choose apple and continue with step 4.

4. Position the mouse pointer on top of the apple, and when the mouse shape changes to a four-headed arrow, drag the apple to the lower-left corner of the slide.

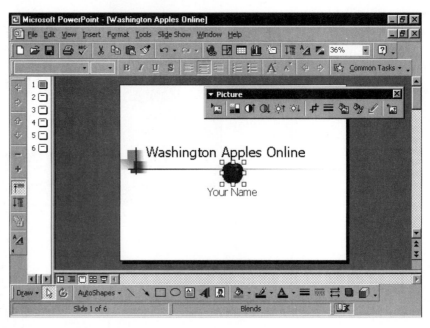

If the Picture toolbar doesn't appear as shown, continue with the instructions as they are written or choose View>Toolbars>Picture.

5. Press Control and drag the apple to the right. Choose copy here.

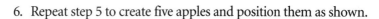

6. Repeat step 5 to create five apples and position them as shown.

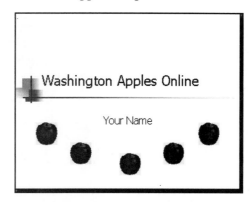

7. Choose Insert>Text Box.

8. Drag to create a text box under the first apple.

9. Type "Apples are…".

10. Select "Apples are…" and change the font size to 20 pt.

11. Repeat steps 7-11 to create the following text boxes:

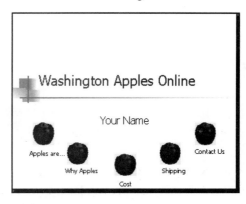

12. Save your presentation.

Inserting Hyperlinks

1. Go to Slide 1.

2. Click on the first apple to select it.

3. Choose Insert>Hyperlink from the Menu bar.

4. Choose Place in This Document under Link to: at the Insert Hyperlink dialog box.

You only need to click once on an object to select it. If you accidentally double-click an object, click off of the object or choose Close and try again.

Control-K is the keyboard shortcut to insert a hyperlink.

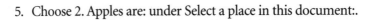

5. Choose 2. Apples are: under Select a place in this document:.

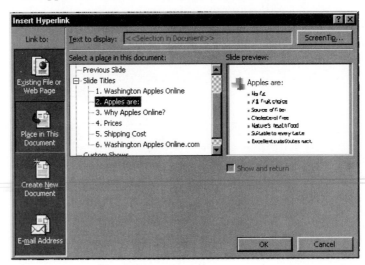

6. Click OK.

7. Click on the Apples are: text box to select it.

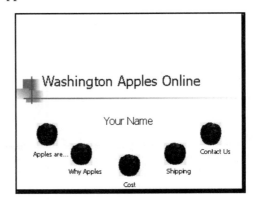

8. Press Control-K.

9. Repeat steps 4-6 to link the text box to Slide 2.

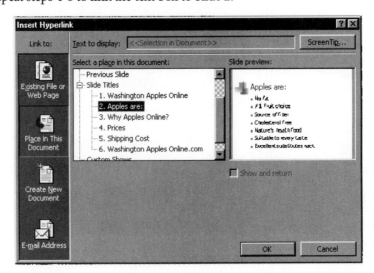

Control-K is the keyboard shortcut to insert a hyperlink.

10. Use this method to link each apple and text box to their appropriate slide.

11. Save your presentation.

Testing Hyperlinks

1. Switch to Slide Show view.

2. Point to each apple or text box.

3. When the shape of the mouse changes to a pointing finger to indicate a hyperlink, click to link to the appropriate slide.

You can also navigate to the previous and next slides by pressing the Left and Right Arrows or by right-clicking and choosing the appropriate option from the menu.

4. To return to Slide 1, right-click and choose Go>Slide Navigator>1. Washington Apples Online and choose Go To.

5. Test each of your hyperlinks.

6. Press Esc to return to Slide view.

7. Go to Slide 1 and type your name in place of "Your Name."

8. Save your presentation.

Adding Web Address Hyperlinks

1. Go to Slide 6.

2. If necessary, resize the title placeholder so that the title appears on one line as shown.

3. Select "Washington Apples Online.com."

4. Click on the Insert Hyperlink button ![icon] on the Standard toolbar.

5. Click on Existing File or Web Page under Link to: at the Insert Hyperlink dialog box.

6. Type "http://www.applesonline.com" in the text box as shown.

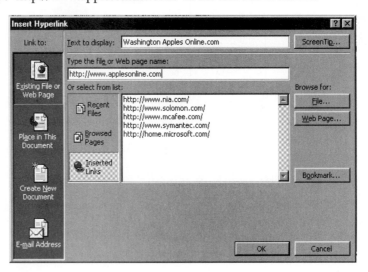

7. Click OK.

8. Save your presentation.

Adding E-mail Addresses

1. Select the E-mail address sales@applesonline.com.

2. Press Control-K.

3. Click on E-mail Address under Link to: at the Insert Hyperlink dialog box.

4. Type "wa@applesonline.com" in the E-mail address text box.

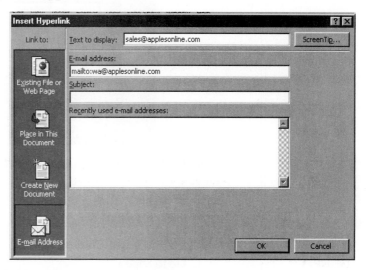

5. Click OK and Save your presentation.

Editing Hyperlinks

1. Select sales@applesonline.com and right-click on the selected text.

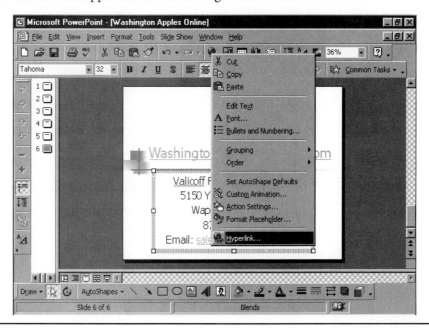

2. Choose Hyperlink>Edit Hyperlink from the shortcut menu that appears.

3. Change the "wa" to "sales".

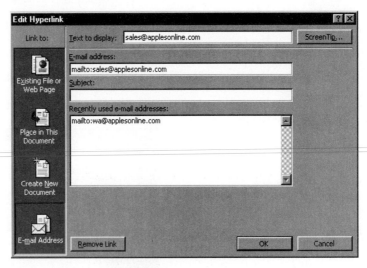

4. Click OK and Save your presentation.

Copying as Hyperlink

1. Go to Slide 1.

2. Select the text "Washington Apples Online" in the title placeholder.

3. Choose Edit>Copy from the Menu bar.

4. Go to Slide 2.

5. Choose Edit>Paste as Hyperlink.

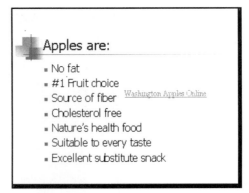

6. Click on the Washington Apples Online hyperlink.

7. Position the four-headed arrow on the border and move the placeholder as shown.

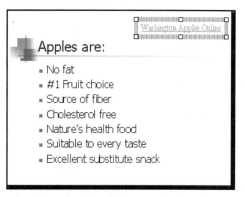

8. Select the text "Washington Apples Online" and choose Insert>Hyperlink.

9. Type "Return Home" in the Text to display text box.

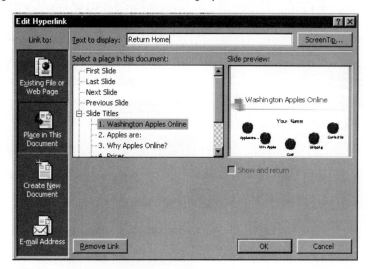

10. Click OK.

11. Move the placeholder to the right.

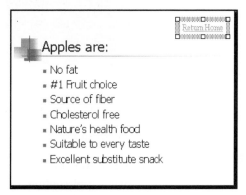

12. Click on the Return to Home text box and press Control-C to copy the text box to the clipboard.

The keyboard shortcut for Copy is Control-C.

To Copy and Paste the text box including the link, you can also use the Copy and Paste buttons on the Standard toolbar or choose Edit>Copy and Edit>Paste from the Menu bar.

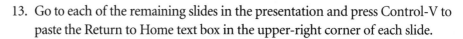

13. Go to each of the remaining slides in the presentation and press Control-V to paste the Return to Home text box in the upper-right corner of each slide.

14. Save your presentation.

Testing Hyperlinks

1. Go to Slide 1.

2. Switch to Slide Show view.

3. Test the internal links on Slide 1 as well as the Return Home links on the other slides.

4. Start your Web browser.

5. Choose File>Open or File>Open Page.

6. Choose Browse or Open and navigate to **Work in Progress** folder.

7. Select the **Project F – Washington Apples Online** file and choose OK or Open to open the Web page in your browser.

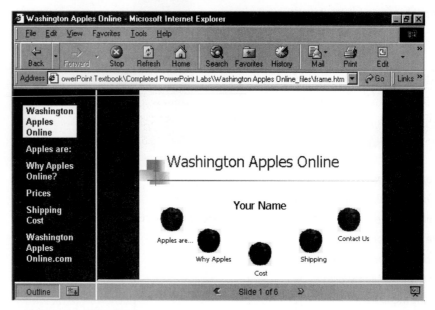

8. Test the hyperlinks in the left frame as well as the hyperlinks on Slide 1 and the Return Home hyperlinks on all slides.

9. Go to Slide 6.

10. Click on Washington Apples Online.com to test the hyperlink to http://www.applesonline.com.

11. Click on the E-mail address on Slide 6.

12. If the browser has been properly configured, an E-mail window should display.

13. If necessary, close the E-mail window and then close your browser.

14. Return to PowerPoint and make any necessary changes to your presentation.

15. Save your presentation.

Publishing Web Pages

1. Choose File>Save as Web Page.

2. Click on the Publish button in the middle of the Save As dialog box.

3. At the Publish As Web Page dialog box, specify the path given to you by your Internet Service Provider.

4. Choose Publish to post your Web page on a server that is accessible to the Internet community.

5. Exit PowerPoint.

To complete these instructions, you must first contact your Internet Service Provider for details regarding how to publish your Web page to a server that is accessible to the Internet community.

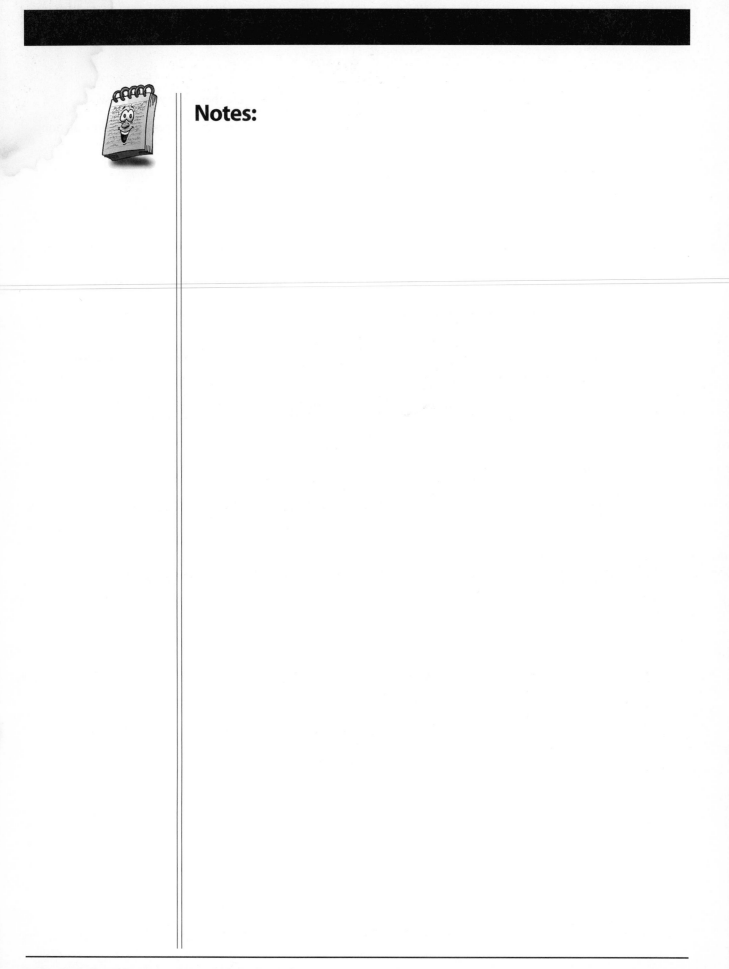

Notes:

Project G: Yard Debris Recycling Program

Adding Speaker Notes

1. Start PowerPoint and choose Open an existing presentation.

2. From the **SF-PowerPoint** open the **Yard Debris Recycling Program** file.

3. Go to Slide 1 and Type your name in place of "Your Name" in the subtitle placeholder.

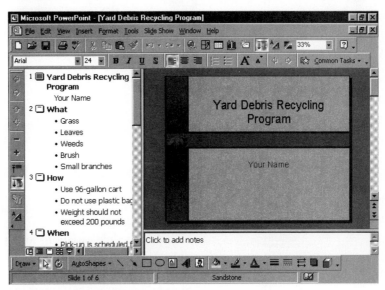

4. Choose View>Notes Page.

5. Click on the drop-down list box next to Zoom on the Standard toolbar and choose 75%.

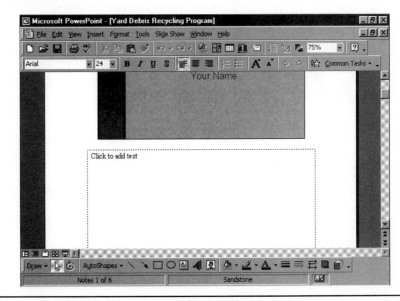

The keyboard shortcut to open an existing presentation is Control-O.

6. Click to add the following text in the Notes area of the page: "Thank customers for signing up". Press Enter and then type "Yard debris recycling is easy and convenient". Press Enter and type "Helping turn yard debris into useful compost".

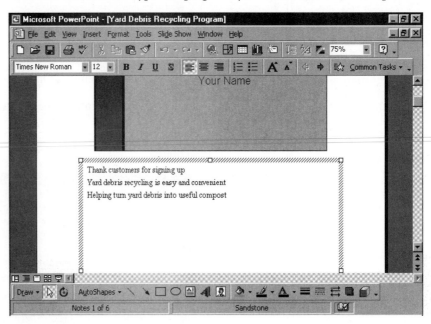

It is not necessary to zoom in to type in the text in the Notes Pages section, but it may be easier to see the text as you type. In addition, you can type the text in the notes area from Normal and Outline views as well as from Notes Page view.

7. Add the following notes to each slide:

   Slide 3: "Remember, wet grass and leaves are heavier, so fill cart accordingly".

   Slide 4: "Schedule variations for winter months will appear on your billing notice".

   Slide 6: "Encourage customers to call if they have questions".

8. Save your presentation into your **Work in Progress** folder as "Project G - Yard Debris Recycling Program".

9. Keep this file open for the following exercises.

Adding Transitions and Animation

1. Go to Slide 1.

2. Switch to Slide Sorter view.

3. Choose Edit>Select All.

4. Click on the Transitions drop-down list box and choose Split Horizontal Out.

5. Click on the Preset Animation drop-down list box and choose Flash Once, Slow.

You can select all of the slides at one time by pressing Control-A.

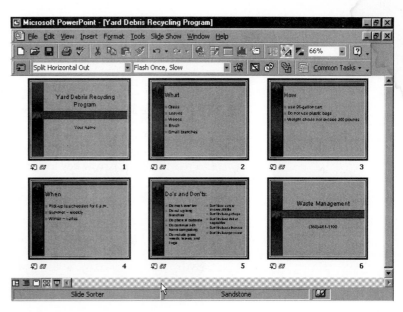

6. Save your presentation.

Start a Slide Show on Any Slide

1. Click on the white background to deselect the slides.

2. Click on Slide 5 to select it.

3. Switch to Slide Show view to start the slide show on Slide 5.

4. Press Esc to return to Slide Sorter view.

5. Switch to Normal view.

6. Go to Slide 2.

7. Choose View>Slide Show to start the slide show on Slide 2.

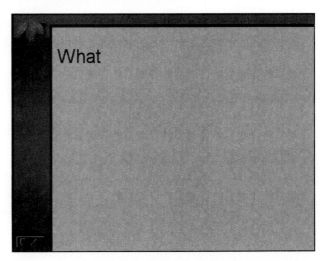

8. Click the left mouse button to view your presentation from Slide 2 to the end.

Navigating a Presentation

1. Switch to Normal view.

2. Go to Slide 3 of your presentation.

3. Switch to Slide Show view.

4. Press the Right Arrow key to see the first bulleted item.

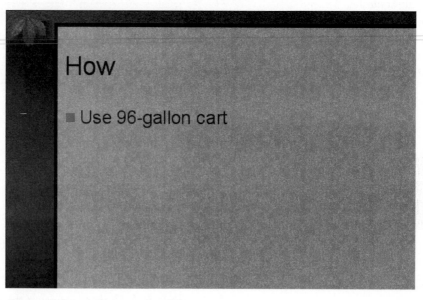

5. Right-click anywhere on the slide.

6. Choose Next to show the second bulleted item.

7. Right-click anywhere on the slide.

8. Point to Go on the Shortcut menu.

9. Choose Slide Navigator.

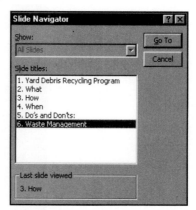

10. Click on Slide 6, Waste Management and choose Go To.

To bring up the Shortcut menu, right-click on the slide or click on the icons in the lower-left corner of the slide.

11. Right-click anywhere on Slide 6.

12. Choose Go>Previously Viewed to return to Slide 3.

13. Right-click anywhere on Slide 3.

14. Choose Go>By Title>5 Do's and Don'ts.

15. Right-click anywhere on Slide 5.

16. Choose End Show to return to Normal view.

Using the Pen Tool

1. Click on Slide 1.

2. Switch to Slide Sorter view.

3. Press Control-A to select all of the slides in the presentation.

4. Change the Preset Animation Flash Once, Slow to Wipe Left.

5. Press F5 to switch to Slide Show view.

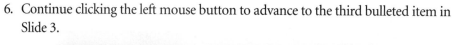

6. Continue clicking the left mouse button to advance to the third bulleted item in Slide 3.

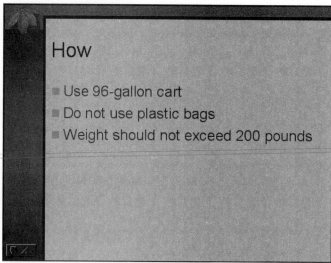

When you use the keyboard shortcut F5 to switch to Slide Show view, PowerPoint automatically starts the slide show on Slide 1.

7. Right-click anywhere on Slide 3 and choose Pointer Options>Pen.

8. Drag a line under "200 pounds".

9. Right-click anywhere on Slide 3.

10. Choose Pointer Options>Automatic, then click the left mouse button to advance to the first bulleted item on Slide 5.

Changing the Pen Tool Color

1. Click on the icon of the slide and arrow in the lower-left corner of the screen.

2. Choose Pen Options>Pen Color>Red.

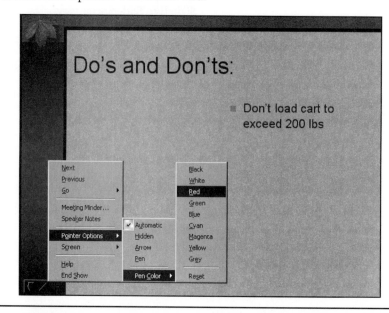

As soon as you advance to the next slide, anything drawn with the Pen tool is erased. You can also erase pen drawings by choosing Screen>Erase Pen.

3. Drag a circle around "200 lbs."

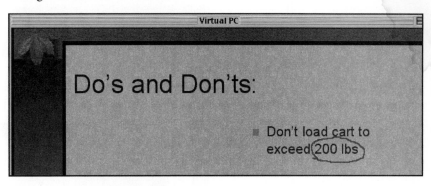

4. Right-click anywhere on Slide 5.

5. Choose Screen>Erase Pen.

6. Right-click anywhere on Slide 5.

7. Choose Pointer Options>Automatic.

8. Click the left mouse button to advance to Slide 6.

Changing the Screen

1. Click on the icon of the slide and arrow in the lower-left corner of the screen.

2. Choose Screen>Black Screen.

3. Right-click on the screen.

4. Choose Screen>Unblack Screen.

5. Click the left mouse button to view the remainder of the presentation and return to Slide Sorter view.

Previewing a Presentation in Black and White

1. Switch to Slide view.

2. Go to Slide 1.

3. Click on the Grayscale Preview button on the Standard toolbar.

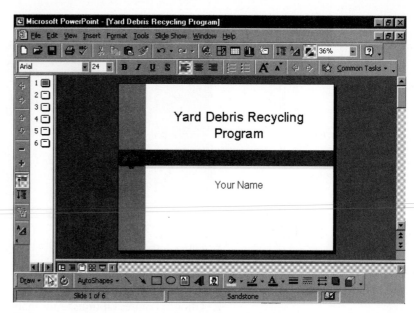

4. Click on the Grayscale Preview button to switch from black-and-white back to color.

Printing Slides

1. Choose File>Print.

2. Click next to Pure black-and-white in the lower-left corner of the Print dialog box to put a check mark in the checkbox as shown.

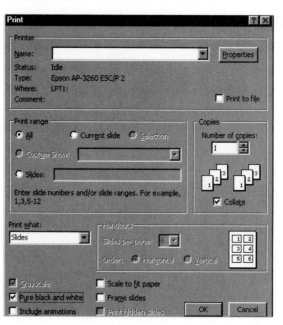

You can also change the preview to and from black-and-white by choosing View>Black and White from the Menu bar.

3. Slides should be selected under Print what:.

4. Click OK to print all six slides of the presentation.

Printing Audience Handouts

1. Press Control-P to access the Print dialog box.

2. Click on the drop-down list box under Print what: and choose Handouts.

3. Set the number of Slides per page to 6 under Handouts.

4. The Pure black-and-white checkbox should be selected.

5. Set the Number of copies to 4.

6. Choose OK to print four, collated copies of audience handouts.

Printing Outlines

1. Choose File>Print.

2. Click on the drop-down list box under Print what:, and choose Outline View.

3. Set the Number of copies to 1.

4. Click OK to print one copy of the outline.

Printing Speaker Notes

1. Go to Slide 1.

2. Choose File>Print.

3. Choose Current slide under Print range.

4. Click on the drop-down list box under Print what:, and choose Notes Pages.

5. Put a check mark in the Grayscale checkbox.

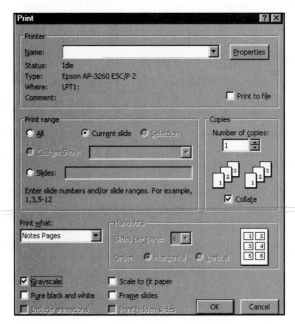

While black-and-white only prints pure black-and-white, depending upon your printer, Grayscale can provide up to 256 different shades of gray.

6. Click OK to print speakers notes for Slide 1.

7. Repeat steps 1-6 to print speakers notes for Slides 3, 4, and 6.

8. Save your presentation.

9. Exit PowerPoint.

GLOSSARY

Animation

On-screen movement as one objects transitions to another object.

Annotations

Notes added to your slides during a presentation.

Arrowheads

The small arrow symbols on the end of the arrow line tool in the graphics tool box.

Attributes

Specific text options, such as font size, style, and color.

AutoContent Wizard

A PowerPoint wizard that allows you to select a presentation type from a list of categories. Based on the category and type of presentation selected, the wizard creates a presentation with sample text that you can customize to meet your own needs.

AutoCorrect

A feature of PowerPoint that automatically corrects misspellings.

AutoLayouts

A slide based on a predefined layout that includes placeholders for text, graphics, charts, tables, bullets, clip art and other media elements .

AutoShape

Predefined shapes such as arrows, cubes, cylinders, hearts, and other objects that can be drawn and manipulated on a slide.

Background

The colored, textured, or blank backdrop on which all slide elements are placed. You might also use photographs or other custom graphics as presentation back-grounds.

Bold

To apply heavier, blacker version to text and other objects.

Bitmap Image

Pixel-based objects that have been created with a Paint program.

Browser

A program that interprets Hypertext Markup Language (HTML) and displays a Web page based on the HTML tags. The two most com-monly used browsers are Internet Explorer and Netscape Navigator.

Bullet

A marker preceding text, usually a solid dot, used to add emphasis; generally indicates that the text is part of a list.

Buttons

Command buttons — such as OK, Cancel, and Print — that allow you to carry out actions.

Cell

The intersection of a column and row in a table.

Checkboxes

A small place in a dialog box that enables you to turn an option on and off by clicking in the space.

Clip Art

A collection of public domain graphics and images.

Clipboard

A temporary location in memory where items that have been cut or copied are stored.

Close button

The button in the upper-right corner of a window that is used to close a window. The close button usually appears as an "x."

Color Scheme

A set of complementary colors professionally designed to work with different media elements used on the slides in a presentation.

Column

The vertical list in a table.

Command button

Buttons from which you can issue commands within a dialog box. OK is an example of a command button.

Control Box

The gray box above the column headings and to the left of the row headings. Control boxes are used to select columns and rows.

Copy

Places a duplicate of an item on the Clipboard for pasting. The original item remains intact.

Copyright

Ownership of a work by the originator, such as an author, publisher, artist, or photographer. The right of copyright permits the originator of material to prevent its use without express permission or acknowledgment of the originator. Copyright may be sold, transferred, or given up contractually.

Cropping

The elimination of parts of an object that are not required.

Cut

Removes an item and stores it on the Clipboard for pasting.

Default

A specification for a mode of computer operation that operates if no other is selected. For example, the default font size might be 12 point, or a default color for an object might be white with a black border.

Demote

To move the level of an item down one step.

Dialog Box

A window in which you provide additional information before a command or task is executed.

Drawing toolbar

PowerPoint toolbar that contains a collection of tools used to create and edit drawing objects,

Effect

The special On-screen movement that occurs as one object moves to another.

Embedded

An object that has been created with another application that is placed on a slide and ultimately becomes part of the PowerPoint presentation.

Emboss

A special effect applied to text to make it appear raised.

Fill

To add a tone or color to the area inside a closed object.

Find and Replace

Feature that automates the process of searching for text and replacing it with different text.

Font

A family or set of characters that share the same design or typeface.

Footer

A fixed body of copy that appears at the bottom of every page of a document.

Format Painter

Tool that allows you to pick up formatting from existing text and apply it throughout your presentation.

Formatting Toolbar

A PowerPoint toolbar that contains the buttons and icons most often used to format text and other slide objects.

Gradient

A fill effect that gradually changes from one color to another.

Grayscale

An image composed in grays ranging from black to white, usually using 256 different shades of gray.

Grouping

When several individual objects are collected together and act as if they were one so that an operation may be applied to all of them simultaneously.

Handles

Small rectangles around a selected object that are used to resize the object.

Handouts

Printed copies of the slides in a presentation that can be distributed to an audience.

Header

A fixed body of copy that appears at the top of every page of a document.

Home Page

The first page of a Web site.

Hyperlink

When text or an object serves as a link or jump to a different location within the same file, to an entirely different file, or to an existing Web or e-mail address.

Hypertext Markup Language (HTML)

Tags interpreted by a Web browser to display a Web page.

Icon

A small graphic symbol used on the screen and activated by clicking the mouse or other pointing device.

Import

To bring a file generated with one application into another application.

Internet

A huge network of networks.

Internet Service Provider (ISP)

A company or organization that provides internet access.

Intranet

An internal, browser-based network.

Italics

Text that has been slanted to the right.

Justification

The alignment of text along margins.

Landscape View

Printing the page in 11-by 8.5 format.

Maximize

To enlarge a window so that it takes up the entire screen.

Media Element

Graphics, sound, animation, or video included on a slide.

Menu Bar

A list at the top of a window that contains command names with drop-down menus or submenus.

Minimize

To reduce a window to a button on the taskbar.

Modem

Hardware device often used to connect a computer to the Internet.

Normal View

The PowerPoint default view. This view contains three panes- outline pane, slide pane, and notes pages pane.

Notes Page View

The PowerPoint view that displays one slide with a text box for speaker notes associated with the slide.

Notes Pane

The area in which you can type speaker notes.

Object

Items that appear on slides including placeholders for text, graphics, charts, video, and other media elements.

Office Assistant

Part of online Help that appears as an interactive and intuitive agent to whom you can pose questions as if you were asking them of a teacher or trainer.

Orientation

A printer setting that designates which edge of the paper should be at the top. The two common orientations are landscape, which is wider than it is tall and portrait, which is taller than it is wide.

Online Help

The help system that is accessible by pressing the F1 key.

Outline Pane

The area on the screen that displays the slide number, icon, and text.

Outline View

The PowerPoint view that emphasizes the outline. In this view the outline pane displays larger than the slide or notes panes.

Paste

When an item that has been cut or copied to the Clipboard appears on a slide.

Pen

Tool used to write on a slide while a presentation is being delivered.

Pixel

A picture element - the smallest dot or unit on a computer monitor or in a bitmapped image.

Placeholder

A container that holds text, graphics, charts, tables, bulleted items, video, animation, and other objects.

Point

A unit of measurement used to specify type size and rule weight, equal to (approximately, in traditional typesetting) 1/72 inch.

Portrait View

Printing the page in 8.5-by 11 format.

Presentation Software

Programs, such as PowerPoint, that are used primarily to created slide shows and On-screen presentations.

Promote

To move the level of an item up one step.

Publishing

The process of posting Web pages to a Web server accessible by the Internet community.

Redo

Undoes the most recently issued Undo command.

Restore

Command that returns a windows to its original size.

Right-Click

Clicking the right mouse button on a Windows system. This is usually used to reveal a shortcut menu.

Rotate

To turn an object at some angle to its original axis.

Row

A horizontal list in a table.

Rulers

Rulers appear along the left and top of the work area, measuring in inches the size of the selected element.

Scale

To reduce or enlarge the amount of space an image with occupy.

Scroll Bar

A bar at the edge of a window that allows you to navigate or move through a window.

Scroll Box

A square box on the scroll bar that you drag to quickly move through a window.

Selecting

The process of placing the cursor over an object and clicking the mouse to make it active.

Shortcut Menu

A menu of commands specific to a particular object or portion of the screen. Shortcut menus generally appears when you right-click on the related object.

Slide Background

The color scheme, patterns, and graphics that appear behind the other media elements on a slide.

Slide Master

The slide that controls the appearance of all the other slides in a presentation.

Slide Pane

The area on the screen that displays the slide.

Slide Show View

The PowerPoint view that displays each slide at full screen. This is the view that is used when a presentation is being delivered to an audience.

Slide Sorter View

The PowerPoint view that displays all of the slides in a miniature format. This view is often used for rearranging, deleting and copying slides, as well as for applying slide transitions and animation.

Slide View

The PowerPoint view that emphasizes the slide. In this view the slide pane displays larger than the outline or notes panes. This view is often used to edit slide content.

Speaker Notes

Reminders used by the speaker during a presentation. Speaker notes are not seen by the audience.

Spelling Checker

Checks the spelling in your presentation.

Standard Toolbar

A PowerPoint toolbar that contains the buttons and icons most often used in PowerPoint. The commands on this toolbar come primarily from the File and Edit commands on the Menu bar.

Status Bar

A PowerPoint toolbar that displays information about the location of the insertion point. This toolbar is located at the bottom of the window.

Subscript

Text that falls below the baseline.

Subtopic

A point that supports a main topic.

Superscript

Text that falls above the baseline.

Tables

A series of intersecting columns and rows which create cells for storing text and other media elements.

Taskbar

The Windows bar that contains the Start menu and icons that represent open applications. It generally appears at the bottom of the screen. .

Template

A preset design scheme that includes colors, fonts, and layout and is applied to all of the slides in a presentation. Templates are easy to use and help you create a consistent, professional presentation.

Text Box

A placeholder for text including titles, bulleted lists, comments, and labels.

Title Bar

The title bar displays the name of the window. It is located at the top of a window. Provided the window is not maximized, you can move the window to another location by dragging the title bar.

Tooltip

A yellow box containing the name of the icon.

Transition

Special effects that display between the slides in a presentation as it is being delivered in Slide Show view.

Underline

Text that is formatted with an line underneath it.

Undo

Reverses the last executed command.

Ungrouping

The breaking apart of one object into several individual objects so that an operation may be applied to each of them independently.

Uniform Resource Locator (URL)

The address of a Web page.

Views

Several different ways to see your presentation that are available: slide view, slide sorter view, outline view, notes pages view, and slide show.

Web Page

An HTML document that can be viewed using a Web browser. A page that is part of the World Wide Web.

Weight

The thickness of the strokes of a typeface, line, or rule.

Wizard

An automated feature that assists you in creating or completing an operation. Wizards ask you to respond to questions, choose from options, and type text.

WordArt

An application that allows you to create decorative text with special effects complete with 3-D and texture.

Word Wrap

The automatic adjustment of the number of words on a line of text to match the margin and hyphenation settings, resulting in shifting a word to the next line as required.

Work Area

The central area of the screen on which you create slides for your presentation.

World Wide Web (Web)

A collection of HTML documents or Web pages that may include text, graphics, animation, sound, video and virtual reality. The Web is an area of the Internet accessible via a Web browser.

Zoom

Process of electronically enlarging an image on a monitor to facilitate detailed design or editing.

INDEX

NOTES

NOTES

NOTES